ployment Records), *In the Case of Hyman Schlesinger,* UE Archives; J. A. Carlson to Mr. Tolson, February 20, 1950, FBI Cvetic.

4. *People of the State of New York by Alfred J. Bohlinger, Superintendent of Insurance v. The International Workers Order, Inc.,* 199 Misc. 941 (hereafter cited as "IWO Trial Record"), pp. 2455, 2462, 2499. The multivolume trial record as well as the appellate record are available in the archives of the International Workers Order, located at the Labor-Management Documentation Center, Martin P. Catherwood Library, New York State School of Industrial and Labor Relations, Cornell University, Ithaca, New York. Cvetic as told to Martin, "I Posed as a Communist," pt. 1, p. 94; "Cvetic, Matthew C." (Background Information in Employment Record), *In the Case of Hyman Schlesinger,* UE Archives.

5. "Deposition of Natalie Mackenzie," in *United States of America v. Steve Nelson* (in the United States District Court for the Western District of Pennsylvania), p. 2, and "Libel and Divorce–Marie D. Cvetic vs. . . . ," pp. 3, 5, both in Schlesinger, Box 139, UE Archives; Govorchin, *Americans from Yugoslavia,* p. 188; James Moore, "Undercover Man 9 Years Tells Inside Story of Area Commies," *Pittsburgh Sun-Telegraph,* February 19, 1950, clipping, FBI Cvetic.

6. *Pittsburgh Post-Gazette,* February 21, 1950, p. 1, clipping, FBI Cvetic; *The American Slav,* January 1939. The *American Slav,* which during Ms. Barsh's tenure was also the "Official Organ of the Slav Athletic Federations," later became the *American Slavonic Review.*

7. "Commonwealth of Pennsylvania vs. Matthew C. Cvetic, . . . Information," *In the Case of Hyman Schlesinger,* UE Archives; Cvetic as told to Martin, "I Posed as a Communist," pt. 1, p. 18 ("She put out her hand to support herself and she fell and broke her wrist"); IWO Trial Record, pp. 2476–79; *Pittsburgh Press,* February 20, 1950, p. 2, and *Pittsburgh Post-Gazette,* February 21, 1950, p. 1, clippings, both in FBI Cvetic. On reporting this incident to Hoover, a Federal attorney seemed somewhat dismayed with Cvetic's concept that "beating up one's in-laws was an American custom" (William F. Tomkins, Assistant Attorney General, Internal Security Division, Department of Justice, to Hoover, May 5, 1955, a multipage letter concerning "Witnesses Used in Subversive Activities Cases," Criminal Division, U.S. Department of Justice, Washington, D.C., Ref No. CRM-890912F).

8. Telephone interview with James Moore, August 12, 1988; SAC Pittsburgh to Hoover, February 16, 1949, FBI Cvetic; "Description of Helen Newman as given by Matt Cvetic to Morris Ebenstein [Warner's executive], August 15, 1950," Box I-45, WB USC. There is a fascinating clip of Cvetic in the 1992 BBC *Timewatch* series, "The Un-American," a well-made, penetrating, useful, but ultimately flawed production whose approach to some very complex post–World War II political issues is overly simplistic.

9. Kenneth O'Reilly, *Hoover and the Un-Americans: The FBI, HUAC, and the Red Menace* (Philadelphia: Temple University Press, 1983), p. 22; Don Whitehead, *The FBI Story: A Report to the People* (New York: Random House, 1956), p. 158. Both the critical O'Reilly and the adulatory Whitehead depend on a Hoover memorandum of the August meeting. Curt Gentry, *J. Edgar Hoover: The Man and the Secrets* (New York: W. W. Norton, 1991), a writer critical of the FBI head, points out (on p. 206) that "exactly what was said in August during this and a subsequent meeting . . . is a matter of dispute, since there is only one record of what occurred: Hoover's own memorandum for the files. In short, there is only Hoover's word for what was said." Athan Theo-

haris, ed., *From the Secret Files of J. Edgar Hoover* (Chicago: Ivan R. Dee, 1991), pp. 179–83, no less a critic of Hoover, gives credence to the Director's memos of the meetings (reprinted in this collection) and the "presidential authorization" that "predicated" FBI antisubversive activity. Athan G. Theoharis and John Stuart Cox, *The Boss: J. Edgar Hoover and the Great American Inquisition* (Philadelphia: Temple University Press, 1988), pp. 185–86.

10. Harvey Klehr and John Earl Haynes, *The American Communist Movement: Storming Heaven Itself* (New York: Twayne, 1992), p. 94; Irving Howe and Louis Coser, *The American Communist Party* (Boston: Beacon Press, 1957), chap. 9; Teamster president Dan Tobin, quoted in Bert Cochran, *Labor and Communism: The Conflict That Shaped American Unions* (Princeton: Princeton University Press, 1977), p. 163; Steven Fraser, *Labor Will Rule: Sidney Hillman and the Rise of American Labor* (New York: The Free Press, 1991), p. 466. Also see Walter Galenson, *The CIO Challenge to the AFL: A History of the American Labor Movement* (Cambridge: Harvard University Press, 1960), p. 185.

11. Foster Rhea Dulles and Melvyn Dubofsky, *Labor in America: A History* (dArlington Heights, Ill.: Harlan Davidson, 1993), p. 314; William A. Turner, *Hoover's F.B.I.* (1970; revised and updated, New York: Thunder's Mouth Press, 1993), p. 182.

12. Richard Gid Powers, *Secrecy and Power: The Life of J. Edgar Hoover* (New York: The Free Press, 1987), p. 295.

13. Philbrick, *I Led Three Lives* (New York: McGraw Hill Book Co., 1952), p. 65; Angela Calomiris, *Red Masquerade: Undercover for the F.B.I.* (Philadelphia: J. B. Lippincott, 1950), p. 15. Mary Mazzei followed in her husband's footsteps in 1943 when she joined the CP at the request of the FBI.

14. Cvetic as told to Martin, "I Posed as a Communist," pt. 1, p. 94; HUAC Cvetic, p. 1196; Hoover to Assistant Attorney General James M. McInerney, December 23, 1950, FBI Cvetic; Cvetic's wife quoted in Mrs. G. Nuss to Hyman Schlesinger, June 13, 1950, *In the Case of Hyman Schlesinger*, UE Archives. Schlesinger represented Nuss at a deportation hearing where Cvetic testified and had a copy of the letter in the files he put together in an effort to discredit Cvetic when he testified against the lawyer in attempted disbarment proceedings. Because Schlesinger was literally fighting for his professional life, his files on Cvetic are a treasure trove. I did not have access to them at the time I was doing the research for my article on Cvetic that appeared in 1991 in *The Pennsylvania Magazine of History and Biography*. Cvetic later informed the Bureau that after being treated for heart trouble in 1930 he some years later learned it was "a heart phobia after consulting a psychiatrist" whom thereafter he "periodically" contacted (Edward Schmidt, SAC New York City, to the Director, February 15, 1949, p. 6, FBI Cvetic).

15. Cvetic as told to Martin, "I Posed as a Communist," pt. 1, p. 94; SAC Pittsburgh to Hoover, February 26, 1942, FBI Cvetic.

16. Cvetic as told to Martin, "I Posed as a Communist," pt. 1, p. 94; SAC Pittsburgh to Hoover, February 16, 1943, FBI Cvetic; HUAC Cvetic, p. 1198; Cvetic as told to Martin, "I Posed as a Communist," pt. 1, p. 19; Cvetic, *The Big Decision*, p. 1.

17. Cvetic as told to Martin, "I Posed as a Communist," pt. 1, p. 19, July 29, 1950, p. 30; Cvetic, "Red Mask," p. 63; HUAC Cvetic, pp. 1196, 1200, 1208; G. C. Callan, SAC Pittsburgh, to A. Rosen, Assistant Director, Washington, D.C., December 7, 1944, and John Edgar Hoover, Director, Federal Bureau of Investigation, to SAC Pittsburgh, December 28, 1944, both in FBI Cvetic.

18. Cvetic as told to Martin, "I Posed as a Communist," pt. 1, p. 17; H. T. O'Connor, SAC Pittsburgh, to Director FBI, April 11, 1945, p. 1, and SAC Pittsburgh to Director FBI, February 15, 1949, both in FBI Cvetic; Cvetic, "Red Mask," p. 84; Cvetic as told to Martin, "I Posed as a Communist," pt. 3, p. 99. Reports are dated as follows: 2-16-43, 6-10-45, 6-12-45, 6-15-45, 7-1-45, 7-15-45, 7-29-45, 7-31-45, 8-18-45, 8-21-45, 1-13-46, 11-17-46, 11-24-26, 12-3-46, 12-9-46, 12-22-46, 2-26-47, 5-5-47, 6-22-47, 6-29-47, 7-13-47, 10-7-47, 10-18-47, 1-15-48, 2-13-48, 4-12-48, 5-6-48 (2), 5-15-48, 5-16-48, 5-26-48, 6-2-48, 6-29-48, 7-1-48, 7-9-48, 7-11-48, 8-7-48, 8-11-48, 8-14-48, 8-26-48, 9-16-48, 10-9-48 (2), 10-12-48, 10-23-48, 11-9-48, 11-30-48, 12-3-48, 12-17-48, 12-20-48, 12-21-48, 12-30-48, 1-12-49, 1-14-49, 1-16-49, 1-19-49, 1-20-49, 1-21-49 (2), 1-23-49, 1-26-49, 2-1-49, 2-7-49 (2), 2-9-49, 2-16-49, 2-16-49 (Steve Nelson), 2-22-49, 3-1-49, 3-2-49 (CP of W. PA), 3-2-49, 3-3-49, 3-8-49, 3-10-49, 3-13-49, 3-14-49, 3-16-49, 3-22-49, 3-25-49, 3-30-49, 4-6-49, 4-7-49, 4-21-49, 4-26-49, 4-29-49, 5-10-49, 5-12-49, 5-18-49, 5-23-49, 6-15-49, 9-10-49, 9-26-49, 11-5-49, 11-13-49, 12-8-49, 12-15-49, 1-7-50, 1-14-50 (Pittsburgh to Bureau, October 10, 1952, pp. 2, 3, FBI Cvetic).

19. H. K. Johnson, SAC Pittsburgh, to Director, June 7, 1943; H. T. O'Connor, SAC Pittsburgh, to Bureau, May 6, 1945; F. A. Fletcher, SAC Pittsburgh, to Director FBI, January 17, 1947, and October 15, 1945; Hoover to F. A. Fletcher, April 14, 1948; Hoover to SAC Pittsburgh, November 24, 1949; J. A. Carlson to Mr. Tolson, February 20, 1950–all in FBI Cvetic.

20. Cvetic, *The Big Decision,* pp. 82, 126, 128; Cvetic as told to Martin, "I Posed as a Communist," pt. 2, p. 53.

21. Cvetic, "Red Mask," pp. 12, 13; Cvetic as told to Martin, "I Posed as a Communist," pt. 1, p. 94; *Pittsburgh Press,* February 19, 1950, in Newspaper Clipping Collection, Pennsylvania Room, The Carnegie Library of Pittsburgh–unless otherwise noted all citations to Pittsburgh newspapers are from this holding (hereafter referred to as "Newspaper Carnegie Pittsburgh"); Jeffrey Zaslow, "When the Red Scare Hit Pittsburgh," *Pittsburgher Magazine,* March 1980, p. 64.

22. Cvetic as told to Martin, "I Posed as a Communist," pt. 1, p. 94; Cvetic, "Red Mask," p. 13.

23. *Pittsburgh Sun-Telegraph,* February 20, 1950, and *Pittsburgh Press,* February 14, 1920; Matthew and Richard Cvetic to Justice Michael Musmanno, August 1, 1962, Cvetic file, Musmanno Papers, Duquesne University (file and holding hereafter cited as "Musmanno Papers"); Zaslow, "Red Scare," p. 64.

24. Ben Cvetic, quoted in Zaslow, "Red Scare," p. 63; SAC Pittsburgh to Hoover, February 16, 1943, FBI Cvetic.

25. Hoover to SAC Pittsburgh, February 23, 1943, and SAC Pittsburgh to Hoover, April 7, 1945, both in FBI Cvetic. The exact schedule of payments was as follows: 1943–$15, $25, $35; 1945–$42.50, $50; 1947–$65; 1948–$85 (Hoover to SAC Pittsburgh: Feb. 22, June 12, Dec. 15, 1943; June 13, Sept. 24, 1945; July 18, 1947; June 3, May 16, Nov. 2, 1948).

26. Patrick Fagan, then head of the U.S. Employment Service in Pittsburgh, quoted in Cvetic as told to Martin, "I Posed as a Communist," pt. 2, p. 54; IWO Trial Record, p. 2677; *Pittsburgh Press,* April 12, 1953; U.S.E.S., Cvetic Employment Record, *In the Case of Hyman Schlesinger,* UE Archives.

27. Cvetic as told to Martin, "I Posed as a Communist," pt. 3, p. 30; "Investigation Procedure, Cvetic," *In the Case of Hyman Schlesinger,* UE Archives; SAC Pittsburgh to Director FBI, May 7, 1950, FBI Cvetic.

28. Artenas C. Leslie, Insurance Commissioner, Commonwealth of Penn-

sylvania, . . . to Hyman Schlesinger, June 16, 1950, "Cvetic," *In the Case of Hyman Schlesinger,* UE Archives; Cvetic as told to Martin, "I Posed as a Communist," pt. 3, p. 30; Nelson to Leab, September 20, 1990, p. 5; SAC Pittsburgh to Hoover, May 7, 1948, p. 3, FBI Cvetic.

29. Stephen Fox, *Blood and Power: Organizational Crime in Twentieth Century America* (New York: William Morrow, 1989), p. 182; Cvetic as told to Martin, "I Posed as a Communist," pt. 1, p. 92.

30. Cvetic as told to Martin, "I Posed as a Communist," pt. 1, p. 92; Steve Nelson, *The 13th Juror—The Inside Story of My Trial* (New York: Masses & Mainstream, 1955), p. 237; Cvetic, *The Big Decision,* p. 68; David Caute, *The Great Fear: The Anti-Communist Purge Under Truman and Eisenhower* (New York: Simon & Schuster, 1978), p. 217.

31. *Pittsburgh Sun-Telegraph,* February 21, 1950, p. 2 (just how much hotel manager Thomas F. Troy actually knew about Cvetic's ties remains open to speculation—Troy may have been taken in at least in part by the manipulative Cvetic. The hotel man told a reporter Cvetic "worked directly out of . . . Washington. The local FBI didn't even know about him"); Cvetic as told to Martin, "I Posed as a Communist," pt. 1, p. 94; interview with Monsignor Rice, August 16, 1988; telephone interview with James Moore, August 12, 1988.

32. "Description of 'Helen Newman,' " as given by Matt Cvetic to Morris Ebenstein, August 15, 1950, Box I-45, WB USC; Cvetic as told to Martin, "I Posed as a Communist," pt. 3, p. 100; Cvetic, "Red Mask," p. 15; SAC Pittsburgh to Hoover, March 1, 1947, FBI Cvetic.

33. Hoover to SAC Pittsburgh, March 17, 1947; D. M. Ladd (Assistant to the Director) to Hoover, March 27, 1947; Hoover to SAC Pittsburgh, March 31, 1947; SAC New York City to Hoover, February 15, 1949—all in FBI Cvetic. Interview with Monsignor Rice, August 16, 1988; telephone interview with James Moore, August 12, 1988; *Pittsburgh Post-Gazette,* June 14, 1946, p. 1.

34. *Pittsburgh Press,* February 19, 1950, p. 1; Cvetic as told to Martin, "I Posed as a Communist," pt. 1, p. 18; *Pittsburgh Press,* February 24, 1950, p. 11, and *Erie Dispatch,* February 23, 1950, clippings, both in FBI Cvetic; U.S. Congress, House of Representatives, Committee on Un-American Activities, *Report on the American Slav Congress . . . ,* June 26, 1949, p. 74.

35. *Pittsburgh Press,* February 24, 1950, p. 11; Nelson, *The 13th Juror,* p. 181; Steve Nelson, James R. Barrett, and Rob Ruck, *Steve Nelson—American Radical* (Pittsburgh: University of Pittsburgh Press, 1981), p. 312; Cvetic, "Red Mask," p. 81; IWO Trial Record, p. 2648.

36. Francis Cardinal Spellman, quoted in Ronald W. Schatz, *The Electrical Workers: A History of Labor at General Electric and Westinghouse* (Urbana: University of Illinois Press, 1983) and in John Cooney, *The American Pope: The Life and Times of Francis Cardinal Spellman* (New York: Times Books, 1984), p. 165; Gino Evora Nicasio, "The Rhetoric of Fulton J. Sheen: A Fantasy Theme Analysis of the Television Speaker in Russia and Communism" (Ph.D. diss., Department of Speech Communications, Indiana University, 1991), p. 198.

37. *Communism: Menace to Freedom—Articles Adapted from Reader's Digest* (Pleasantville, N.Y.: Reader's Digest Services, 1962); Arthur J. Sabin, *In Calmer Times: The Supreme Court and Red Monday* (Philadelphia: University of Pennsylvania Press, 1999), p. 29; Nelson, Barrett, and Ruck, *Steve Nelson,* p. 302.

38. *Pittsburgh Press,* April 3, 1949, pp. 1f.; Nelson, Barrett, and Ruck, *Steve Nelson,* p. 303; Cvetic as told to Martin, "I Posed as a Communist," pt. 3, p. 99.

MIND MAGIC

Reprinted in 2011
First published in 2003 by New Holland Publishers (UK) Ltd
London • Cape Town • Sydney • Auckland

Garfield House, 86-88 Edgware Road, London W2 2EA, United Kingdom
www.newhollandpublishers.com

80 Mckenzie Street, Cape Town 8001, South Africa

Unit 1, 66 Gibbes Street, Chatswood, NSW 2067, Australia

218 Lake Road, Northcote, Auckland, New Zealand

11 13 15 17 19 20 18 16 14 12

ISBN 978 1 84330 476 0

Publishing Manager: Jo Hemmings
Project Editor: Camilla MacWhannell
Editor: Trish Burgess
Illustrator: Phil Garner
Cover Design and Design: Alan Marshall and Gülen Shevki
Production: Joan Woodroffe

Printed in China by Leo Paper Group

Photograph of author on p6 by Rob Thompsett

MIND
MAGIC

EXTRAORDINARY TRICKS TO
MYSTIFY, BAFFLE AND ENTERTAIN

MARC LEMEZMA

NEW HOLLAND

CONTENTS

PREFACE

Whether you choose to believe in psychic phenomena or not, there is no question that there is much that mankind cannot explain with ease. Wherever there is a mystery, you will find those who seek answers, and for every one 'seeker' you will find ten who are simply willing to accept and believe totally.

If we use this knowledge to our advantage, it becomes possible for us to create true wonder in the minds of our audience. If they are willing to believe, or put another way, willing to suspend their disbelief, then half your work is done. They have already begun to convince themselves that what they are witnessing is not the work of an illusionist, but the work of forces unknown.

In my work as a professional magician and entertainer I have the good fortune to work with audiences of all types and all ages – and in many styles. One day I can be performing colourful, fun magic to a group of five-year-olds at a birthday party, the next I can be entertaining a group of businessmen with polished sleight of hand over dinner. While both are satisfying, I feel more at home in the territory covered by this book – mind magic.

Mind magic sits on the border between regular magic tricks and the inexplicable. It is not simply mind-reading, or mentalism as it is known, but a combination of this with strange physical experiments. Mind magic is most definitely not about the use of evil forces or collusion with the Devil. It is simply an entertainment, just like the magic of David Copperfield. The key difference between the two is the level of belief you seek to instill in the audience.

This belief is created in many ways: by the style of your performance, the clothes you wear, your choice of words, the props you use and, most critically, the time and place you choose to perform.

This book begins with some simple tricks to get you started as a mind-magician. It then takes you through other, more subtle, concepts, leading up to how you can go about holding your own paranormal party – purely for fun, of course.

While I choose to believe in the supernatural, you might not. Whatever your views, I hope you enjoy this short foray into the dark, deep and intriguing world of the paranormal and mind magic.

Marc Lemezma

INTRODUCTION

We begin with a story…

Long, long ago, a small group of our distant ancestors was watching the night sky, awe-struck by the sights above.

They marvelled at the dazzling array of lights and shapes, and sought to find meaning in this heavenly display. Surely it must be a message from the gods? No! It was, they decided, the gods dancing for them. After a good few hours' gazing, they lay down in their crude huts and went to sleep, safe in the knowledge that someone somewhere was looking out for them.

One night a member of the group was restless, and stayed up a little later than the others. Something was troubling him. Suddenly he was struck with an amazing thought. The light-show in the sky repeats itself, not every day, not always the same, but there is a pattern.

After a little more thought and a lot more watching, he could tell his friends what was going to happen during the coming nights. He knew which gods would be in the sky and when. As his predictions came true, the others began to treat him differently. He must be special, favoured by the gods and blessed with divine knowledge.

The observant one became powerful and respected in his tribe. Any problems or questions would be put to him for his opinion, and his words of advice followed closely. He also got the best food available and his choice of mates. This was not a bad thing, perhaps, as he was probably of above average intelligence for his time and could therefore produce good-quality offspring.

✴ Magic Through the Ages

Now, it may not have happened exactly like that, but those who could see order in the world around them and make sense of their environment would clearly thrive.

One question I have always pondered is this. What if we were to tell that ancient thinker that the stars are not in fact gods, but huge balls of gas and fire, a trillion times larger than his village, floating in an infinite void? He would think we were crazy.

Throughout history fact and fantasy have become intertwined as human beings search for answers and often find the truth far stranger than the fiction.

In the past many leaders relied upon wizards, wise men and seers to give them insight and thus aid their decisions, military or otherwise. A fine, albeit mythical example, of such a person was Merlin, magician to King Arthur.

Unfortunately, the path has not always been smooth for those with 'special abilities'. Frequently controlled and pursued by those in power, their ability to predict the future posed a threat to the leaders' absolute authority. In medieval times witches were supposedly burnt at the stake. (In fact, most convicted witches in England were hanged.) The increasing numbers of these poor souls coming before his court began to trouble one sixteenth-century justice of the peace. Reginald Scot was a devout Christian and stated that these 'certeine old women' could not possibly be responsible for plagues, poor harvests, healing, controlling the weather or any of the feats attributed to them.

In his book *The Discoverie of Witchcraft* (1584), Scot wrote: 'But certeinlie, it is neither a witch, nor a divell, but a glorious God that maketh the thunder.' In this text he set out to prove that witches possessed no special powers, and explained at length their rituals and the means by which they deceived. Although its purpose was to debunk rather than instruct, the book became the first in the English language to show how magic tricks could be performed by sleight of hand and other mechanical means.

While the book had its supporters, it was not welcomed by everyone. King James, for example, had it banned and decreed that all copies should be burnt. Nonetheless, it had a dramatic effect on magic and mysticism, acting as a catalyst in the development of conjuring as both art and entertainment. Indeed, you probably wouldn't be reading this book now if it were not for Reginald Scot.

✦ Mental Magic

Since the eighteenth century, magic of all kinds has become almost universally acceptable. Modern-day witches and psychics are not persecuted, although they are still not totally trusted either. However, in the last fifty years or so there has been an enormous growth of interest in magic and mysticism – just look at all the psychic fairs, weird shops, television shows and magazines devoted to these subjects.

This interest has been good for magicians, and we have developed our art to reflect it. This is particularly true of mentalism (mind-reading, thought transference and prediction) and bizarre magick (similar to mentalism, but with more supernatural and occultist themes, plus a lot of theatre to create a truly intense atmosphere). Great mentalists of the past have included Theo Anneman, while current exponents include Max Maven and Larry Becker. In the field of bizarre magick Tony Andruzzi has been influential, and the most astounding exponent today is Dr Marcus.

Practitioners of mentalism and bizarre magick truly bridge the gap between what is seen as conjuring tricks and what may be real magic. Indeed, it can be very difficult to distinguish between a good mentalist or bizarrist and a real psychic.

If I were forced to put a label on the magic in this book, I would say it is a mixture of mentalism and bizarre magick. If you pushed me really hard, I would admit it is 'lite' bizarre magick, for, as you will see, the drama and storytelling makes the difference.

Here in the twenty-first century sophisticated methods of communication have made the world a smaller place: they certainly make it easier to share ideas. This is true in all sorts of fields, not least among people with spiritual and magical beliefs. Centuries of history and culture may have changed some of the names and characters, but the beliefs are essentially the same.

While much remains to be explained in our universe, I strongly believe there is a place for mind magic in our lives, and I have three main reasons for this belief.

First, it is entertaining. People are drawn into this fascinating world and see real results, by which I mean they will believe a mind has been read or a distant image received clairvoyantly.

Second, it is respectful to the world of real magic and the paranormal that many people have faith in. Although from time to time I have used a little licence, I have endeavoured to explain things in the correct terms. Certainly when performing the magic in this book you should be clear whether you are reading a mind or showing evidence of precognition, and I have given you the information to do just this.

Third, mind magic is a bridge. In some ways I hope that in using this book your interest and understanding of magic of all kinds will develop and grow. Whatever path life takes you on, being able to entertain or simply being more aware of the world and people around you can be fantastic assets.

✦ Before You Begin

As you read through this book and experiment with the material you find, I want you to bear one important thing in mind. There is no denying that all the experiences described are brought about through trickery, but when you perform any of these tricks you are a magician – a special individual with special responsibilities.

There are a few rules of magic I would like to share with you, and I strongly recommend you to follow them closely. If you do not, you risk making a fool of yourself and possibly spoiling the chances of any magician your audience might meet in the future. If you follow the rules, which are explained in detail on page 93 and briefly outlined below, you will no doubt give a strong performance that will leave a powerful and lasting impression on your audience.

Rule 1

Practice makes perfect, so make sure you have rehearsed thoroughly.

Rule 2

Never repeat a trick to the same audience.

Rule 3

Never reveal your methods to anyone except other magicians.

So let's get down to business: your first mind magic experience.

FIRST STEPS INTO THE UNKNOWN

'Only the unknown frightens men. But once a man has faced the unknown, that terror becomes the known.'

ANTOINE DE SAINT-EXUPÉRY (1900–44)

It is said that if you were to ask a hundred people what their greatest fear is, most would say not the dark, pain, or even death. Most would tell you it is speaking in public. Being the focus of an audience's attention means that any mistake you make is exposed to everyone. On the other hand, any success is equally revealed, and your skill will be known to all.

This first chapter looks at three straightforward tricks to get you started with mind magic. They need not be performed as a show, but perhaps instead as an aside at any gathering. None requires great skill, so this will allow you to concentrate on putting on a good show and thus build your confidence. From then on your performances will be plain sailing.

Nevertheless, do not be misled into believing that the simplicity of these introductory tricks means they will have a limited impact upon your audience. Indeed, each one on its own is a minor miracle.

★ ★ ★ PREDICTABLE BEHAVIOUR ★ ★ ★ ★

Perhaps one of the most useful weapons in the mind-magician's arsenal is a technique known as 'forcing'. Quite simply, although your spectator believes he or she has had a completely free and unrestricted choice from a number of random items, you have, in fact, severely limited his options.

For example, if I were to ask you to think of any odd number from 50 to 99, I have already limited your choice by half. Later, when I say, 'You had a free choice of a number between 50 and 99. Is that correct?' You cannot deny it is the truth. Yet it seems to any onlooker that you had twice as many choices as you had in reality.

Later in the book, you will see a more complex example of forcing, but for now let's start with an experiment using a very simple force involving a playing card to create the impression of amazing precognition.

You will need

★ *An ordinary deck of cards prepared beforehand for the occasion.*

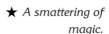

★ *A short note tailored to suit your chosen friend and the situation you will be in.*

★ *A group of friends.*

★ *A smattering of magic.*

✦ The Trick

You and a group of friends are sitting around the open fire in an old English country pub. It is late in the evening and everyone is feeling very relaxed. One of your group returns from the bar with a tray of drinks and hands them out. Your friend Michael reaches for his pint of beer. You turn to Michael and place your hand firmly on his shoulder.

'You know, Michael, you are a true friend. And what I like best about you is your dependability, no, your predictability. You are always there for us, Michael. Let's face it, you come to this pub almost every Friday evening without fail, and you

never need to be asked what you want to drink – always a pint of beer. Tomorrow you will go to the football, Sunday you will spend with your girlfriend, and Monday it's back to work, 8.30 sharp.'

Then, from a pocket, you take a small envelope that has 'To Michael' written across the front. You ask him not to open it yet while you remove a deck of playing cards from their case and begin to shuffle them. You lay the cards on the table in front of Michael and ask him to cut them anywhere he chooses.

You now instruct him to open the envelope and read the note inside, aloud.

'Dear Michael,' he begins, 'I have already explained this evening how much I value your friendship and your dependability. You will be aware that I sometimes see things others do not, so it will not surprise you that I am more aware of your predictability than you are.

'I have already predicted where you will be tonight, what you will choose to drink and your plans for the next few days. Not particularly mystifying, I would agree, but I have also predicted which card you would cut to.

'Michael, you have cut to the king of clubs – a truly confident and dependable card if ever I saw one.'

Michael laughs a touch dismissively and takes a mouthful of beer. One of your other friends leans forward and turns over the card Michael cut to. The entire gathering is covered in beer as Michael splutters in amazement. It is the king of clubs.

✦ Behind the Scenes

You forced Michael to choose the king of clubs using a very straightforward technique called the 'cross-cut force'. This works as follows.

Place your force card, which could be the king of clubs or whichever card you feel is appropriate for your audience, at the very top of the deck. Make sure the back of the force card is uppermost, as shown below.

When the deck was cut, you directed your friend to place the cards he had removed on the table next to the pile of cards that remained. You then asked him to place those remaining cards (cards that were originally the bottom portion of the deck) on top of and at right angles to the cards he had originally cut off, as in the diagram overleaf.

To make the force work you needed to create a little misdirection. More specifically, you needed to make your audience forget which order the piles of cards were originally in and how they had been subsequently laid out. But once you had messed with their memory a little, you simply lifted off the upper portion of the deck and asked Michael to 'pick up the card you cut to'. In fact, this was a complete lie, as you were holding the card he had cut to in your hand. What you actually had him do was turn over the card that was originally on top of the deck – the force card.

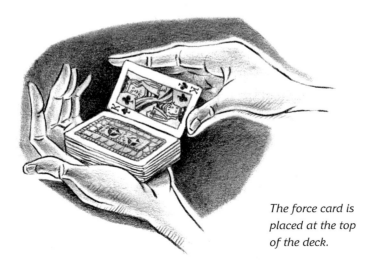

The force card is placed at the top of the deck.

✦ The Performance

To perform this trick with consummate ease, you will need something not so easy to find – the right moment. It would be all too simple to call up your friends right now and say, 'Hey, I've just learnt this great new trick. You've got to get over here and see it.' With mind magic, timing is everything, so judge your time wisely. Everyone needs to be relaxed and have no suspicion of any contrivance on your part. If you do go to the same place each week, you need not perform the trick as soon as you have learnt and prepared it. You may let two or three weeks pass before you decide, 'This is the moment.'

The final stage of the cross-cut force.

So, now you have chosen your moment, you begin to speak to your audience and, in particular, your chosen friend. You hand over the envelope containing your prediction, ask him not to read it yet as you need him to choose a card. Take out your cards and begin to shuffle – this is optional, and a sneaky false shuffle, which keeps your force card on top, is explained later in the book (*see* page 35). Lay the cards in front of him and ask him to cut them. Then place the top half of the deck to one side and sit the bottom half on top of it at right angles. Your force is now set up.

Next comes the misdirection. Until now, all the attention has been on you and the cards, but that is about to change. You ask your friend to open the envelope and read the letter out loud. The attention shifts to him for a minute or two. When you finally draw your audience's attention back to the cards and lift off the upper section of the deck, they will have completely forgotten which half is which. They will accept without question that this was the card your helper cut to, and will be astounded when they see it matches your prediction.

✦ Final Thoughts

Although the method used for this trick is very simple, it is extremely powerful if delivered correctly. Remember: timing is everything. I also think this trick illustrates a lot of basic principles that can be used to enhance your mind magic, so it is an excellent starting point.

You can, of course, be creative in your presentation by choosing interesting combinations of audience, venue and card. I don't know your friends – you do – so give it a little thought.

★ ★ ★ ★ RING-A-RING ARISES ★ ★ ★ ★

Many people might make the assumption that mind magic is simply about reading thoughts, foretelling the future, or perhaps controlling someone's behaviour. While these are all undoubtedly important aspects of mind magic, there is another perspective to the art – the effect of the mind on inanimate objects. This is the dimension we are about to explore, a strange place where objects move mysteriously and apparently unaided by any normal means. This is the power of telekinesis.

You will need

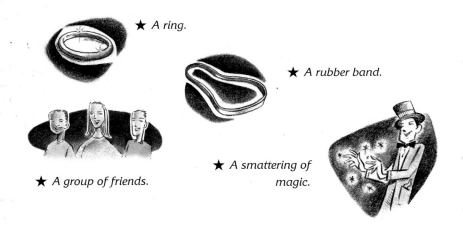

★ A ring.

★ A rubber band.

★ A group of friends.

★ A smattering of magic.

✳ The Trick

As the murmurs die down following the shock of your prediction for Michael, his girlfriend Amanda removes a tissue from her bag and begins to mop up the puddle of beer he spilt on the table in front of everybody. You gaze for a moment at her hand and touch it lightly. 'My word, that's an attractive ring you're wearing. May I take a closer look?' After a small struggle with her finger, she removes the ring and places it in the palm of your hand.

'Very nice indeed. This is quite an old ring, I believe. Did it once belong to a relative now deceased?'

Amanda nods and explains how it was left to her by Joan, her late grandmother.

'Perhaps you have felt something of your departed grandmother's spirit in this ring. I can certainly feel it, and it seems to want to rejoin her now…

'If only the ring had enough energy, it would, I feel, surely wish to find its way

back to its original owner, wherever she may be. What we need to help it on its way is to make a path of minimal resistance. I have an idea!'

You remove a small packet of envelopes from your pocket, which are held together with a rubber band. You take off the band and stretch it back and forth a few times, examining it intently. 'This should do nicely. Please watch carefully and quietly – and concentrate with me.'

You thread Amanda's ring on to the band, then stretch it out between your hands. Your left hand is lower than your right, making a definite incline between the two. The ring sits a little less than one-third of the way up the band.

'Amanda, will you please describe you grandmother to us?'

Everyone listens intently as Amanda paints a vivid picture of Joan: 'She was quite tall and very elegant, always well dressed. She had deep blue eyes and a warm smile…'

'That's very good, Amanda,' you say. 'I want everyone here now to fix that picture of Joan in their mind – beautiful, warm and elegant – and I want you to see her wearing this ring. Amanda, please would you share with us some more memories you might have of Edith.'

Amanda begins to recall distant thoughts of summer holidays at her grandmother's home in the country, of high teas and bedtime stories. At first the memories come thick and fast, but then she begins to slow a little and stutter as the ring begins to quiver gently and starts to make its way along and upwards on the outstretched band. 'I think Joan's ring shares those memories. It seems to want to climb to heaven so that it can be with her again.'

As the ring reaches three-quarters of the way up the rubber band, you glance at Amanda. You see she's becoming quite emotional, touched by this strange experience. You pause, smile and hand the ring back. 'I think this ring belongs here with you, Amanda. Thank you for sharing your memories of Joan. Cherish them always, won't you?'

✳ Behind the Scenes

This can be an amazing experience, yet it almost works itself as it is part physics and part optical illusion. In fact, the ring never moves – not one millimetre. It is the rubber band that moves, under your control of course. Given a little practice in front of a mirror, you can create the appearance of motion and make the experience feel quite eerie.

In general, whatever objects you perform mind magic with, it is important that they look perfectly ordinary, so start by choosing a rubber band of the right colour, length and thickness for the job. Bright colours, such as blue or red, are not ideal, but good old brown rubber bands are perfect. Try to find some that will comfortably stretch to about 60 cm (2 ft) long. Width is not critical, but anything wider than about 3 mm (⅛ in) would be a little unwieldy.

For the rest of the explanation I will assume you are right-handed. If you are left-handed, you simply need to swap hands while you undertake the ring rise.

Thread the rubber band through a ring and pinch one end of the band between your right thumb and forefinger. Make sure you grip this end very firmly. With your left thumb and forefinger, pinch the band tightly about halfway along its length, leaving the remainder of the band resting in your left hand. The ring should be positioned on the section of band between your two hands.

Now stretch the band out between your hands as far as it will go, at the same time raising your right hand a few centimetres higher than your left so as to make a definite incline. Make sure you keep a tight grip with both hands. Gently shake the band to adjust the position of the ring so that it sits perhaps a quarter of the way along, nearest to your left hand.

Now comes the secret moves, which, when combined, produce the effect of movement. The first of these is 'slipping'.

Gently release the pressure between your left thumb and forefinger, thus allowing the band remaining inside your hand to slowly slip through. The section of band stretched between your hands will become longer, but more importantly, the ring will appear to be moving away from your left hand and upwards along the band.

The second secret move is called 'slacking'. Grip tighter again with your left thumb and finger, then gently bring your right hand towards the left, just a little. This slackens the band and compensates for the apparent increase in its length. It also has the effect of making the ring appear to be getting closer to the right hand, further enhancing the illusion of movement.

Given a little practice, you will be able to slip and slack simultaneously, giving the impression of a very smooth and spooky motion when, in fact, the ring never moves at all.

✴ The Performance

Perhaps the most important thing to remember when performing this trick is that the sequence of events is critical to the overall impact.

Begin by showing interest in your friend's ring, and try to get as much information as you can about it. Borrow it, examine it intently and compliment the owner on its beauty. If it is a modern ring, you might want to explain how it will always want to gravitate towards its owner (rising to heaven is not relevant with a modern ring).

Whatever you do, make sure you have created interest in the ring before you bring out the rubber band. Also, try to have it in your pocket for a credible purpose. In Amanda's case, the band was around some envelopes, which will actually be used in the next trick. The band must appear insignificant: if it looks like you had it ready for this occasion, the effect of the trick could be diminished.

Therefore, at no point during your performance should you mention the band – it is just there.

In this trick actions will speak louder than words. Thread the ring on to the band and position yourself to perform the secret moves. Make sure, of course, that you have hidden the remaining portion of the band in your left hand and that no one is viewing from an angle where they can see what you are doing. Focus everyone's attention on the ring and let them see it rise.

This trick is different from the previous one in that there is no definite climax as the ring never makes it to the very top, yet in Predictable Behaviour the moment of revelation is quite astounding. Thus, as it apparently reaches three-quarters of the way along the band, you pause for a moment, look at your friend and hand the ring back, saying that it clearly belongs to her, and perhaps we 'shouldn't disturb her Grandmother's spirit'. Thus we have a moment of drama to provide a definite conclusion to the effect.

✦ Final Thoughts

Performing 'Ring-a-ring Arises' teaches us a valuable lesson about magic in general. You may well have heard the term 'misdirection' used to describe the way in which a magician directs your attention away from something he doesn't want you to see. On stage this could be a flash or a bang, but in a situation with friends a more subtle form of misdirection is used.

All the attention is placed on the ring: the rubber band is never actually mentioned. It just happens to be there around some envelopes, and is of no significance at all. When the ring moves, even if those in your audience believe they know how it was done, the rubber band is less likely to be in their minds. It's a perfect illusion.

One final note. Rings are usually treasured personal items, often quite valuable. Treat the ring you borrow with great care and respect, and never do this trick in an environment where the ring could become lost if dropped.

★ ★ ★ ★ WHOSE LIFE IS IT ANYWAY? ★ ★ ★ ★

When Joseph Niépce invented photography in 1826, mankind took a great step forward. This invention allowed specific moments in time to be recorded accurately and quickly and captured exactly what was happening in the world.

Of course, there were those who had a means to do that already. Psychics and mystics believe in a phenomenon known as psychometry, where inanimate objects 'record' information from the environment around them and replay it in the form of vibrations. By simply holding a personal object in their hands, psychics claim to be able to determine who owns it, and other personal information related to the owner's past, present and future.

This following exercise is an experiment in psychometry that, given a little acting on your part, will leave people talking about your wonderful insight.

You will need

★ *A small personal object borrowed from each person.*

★ *Three envelopes craftily prepared.*

★ *A group of friends.*

★ *A smattering of magic.*

✦ The Trick

The evening at the pub is drawing to a close, many of the customers having taken their coats and set off home. However, a small group of onlookers has gathered around you and your friends, intrigued by the gasps and sounds of amazement coming from your table. You seem ready to leave, but you reluctantly give in to the calls for you to 'Show us just one more, please!'

You pause for a moment, sigh and then begin: 'You may wonder how I was able to tell so much about what Michael was going to do, or how Amanda's ring

managed to move itself. Well, every one of us and every single object is able to receive, store and give off energy. This energy is what I put to use, and I should like to try this one more time before I go.'

Scanning the assembled audience, you say, 'I need three of you to help… Amy, James and Matthew, would you help, please?' They nod, a little uncomfortably.

'Do you all have a small personal item about you? Maybe some jewellery or money, for example? That's good, but don't tell me what they are.'

You pick up the packet of envelopes you left lying on the table earlier and remove two, which have addresses and stamps on them.

'Always bills to pay,' you remark as you put these envelopes away and pick up the remaining three, handing one each to your helpers.

'In a few moments I shall leave the room for a short while. What I would like you then to do is put something small that belongs to you in your envelope and seal it down. When you are finished, please hand the envelopes to Michael for safe-keeping.'

You leave the room for perhaps two or three minutes, returning to find Michael clutching a handful of envelopes and everyone talking expectantly.

'Now, Michael, listen carefully. I want you to hand me the envelopes one at a time in any order you wish.'

He hands you the first. You take it and hold it against your forehead with your eyes lightly closed. 'Hmmm, very interesting. I am getting a good vibration from this.' You place the envelope on the table in front of you and say, 'The next one, please, Michael,' and repeat the process with the second and third envelopes.

Eventually, all three lie in front of you, but you seem uncertain about their content because you hold one or two against your head again.

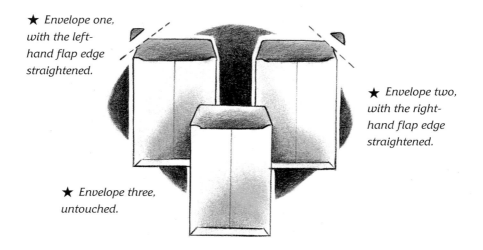

★ Envelope one, with the left-hand flap edge straightened.

★ Envelope two, with the right-hand flap edge straightened.

★ Envelope three, untouched.

'Now I know!' you announce. 'This first envelope has the vibrations of a young man within it. I believe it is yours, James.' You tear open the envelope and tip out a credit card with James's name embossed on it. 'Yours, I believe...' James nods and laughs.

'Well, James, I have often worried about the relationship you have with your credit card. I am not surprised you see it as a very personal item.

'Now we have two envelopes left. Whose is whose, I wonder?'

You gaze at the two remaining envelopes and ponder. You swap them about from left to right, trying to decide which belongs where. You pick one up and look Matthew straight in the eye. 'This envelope is giving me a very clear vibration now. I am picking up the energy of someone full of life and energy at the moment. I know you have not been well lately, Matthew, so I know this belongs to Amy.'

You open the envelope and tip out Amy's engagement ring. When you hand over the final envelope to Matthew you touch him on the shoulder: 'This is yours. I know you will feel stronger soon.'

The group now breaks up as people make their way home, all talking intently about the intriguing and astonishing experiences they have witnessed.

✦ Behind the Scenes

The secret is so simple that it's almost obvious, yet it fools people every time. The envelopes are marked (in a devilishly undetectable manner).

The diagram explains virtually all you need to know. Plain brown envelopes are best, as they do not show up any dirt or finger marks you might leave while preparing them. Make sure they are large enough to accommodate a few coins, a ring, a watch or whatever.

With a sharp craft knife and a ruler simply straighten the diagonal edges of the flaps on the envelope. Designs of envelope vary, so the diagram gives an exaggerated example for you to adapt.

For each performance you will need to make a set of three envelopes.

Put these envelopes in your pocket, perhaps with one or two other letters, and you are all set.

✦ The Performance

This effect really benefits from the suspense and byplay you create. It would be all too easy simply to hand the three envelopes out to their owners immediately, but any impact would be completely lost.

Begin by explaining about psychometry and vibrations, and select your three helpers. It's worth choosing people whom you know at least a little because your knowledge of them will help you to stretch out your revelations. It also helps if you don't choose three people who are sitting right next to each other (they will be less tempted to swap envelopes).

Ask if they have a small personal object on them, but make sure they don't show you before you leave the room. Hand out the three envelopes, making sure you remember who gets which one.

Upon your return, ask for each envelope, determine which is which by virtue of the doctored flaps. The tricky work is now complete: all you need do is play-act.

When you have acted for a while, hand over the first envelope to the appropriate person, explaining why you think it's theirs. Next hold out the second envelope and pause. The suspense can be built by addressing the wrong person, as we did with Matthew in the story. You must decide from what you know of your helpers how to play this part.

Finally, you have to hand the third envelope back. This could be seen as an anti-climax, so again you have to use your wiles to work out something interesting or poignant to say to your third person. You might want to open their envelope and use the enclosed item to help with this. For example, if it contained some money, you might say, 'I could have guessed you would have been motivated by money without being a mind-reader.' Then give a wry smile, creating some uncertainty as to whether you are joking or not.

✦ Final Thoughts

This trick teaches valuable lessons about timing and influencing your audience's attention. You should attempt to convey the impression that you are a caring and sensitive person. Your comments to the helpers, such as those made to Matthew, can easily be taken the wrong way. So be warm and your audience will warm to you.

I KNOW WHAT YOU'RE THINKING!

'Other men are lenses through which we read our own minds.'

RALPH WALDO EMERSON (1803–82)

Now that your appetite has been whetted and you have been given simple things to build your confidence, we can move on to something a little more involved.

One of the most common questions for anyone who claims to be psychic or able to read minds is, 'OK, so what am I thinking right now?'

I usually answer, 'You're thinking that you can catch me out.' This is invariably the case, although they may have other thoughts as well, but they would just love to prove me wrong.

It would clearly be very difficult for someone simply to read all the minds around him. There would be so much going on that it would not be possible to pick on any one thing. It is necessary to focus, concentrate and pick up on individual thoughts, not try to read minds.

Look at the following selection of mind- and thought-reading feats.

★ ★ ★ ★ LIE DETECTOR ★ ★ ★ ★

Magic spectators can be divided into roughly three camps:

★ Those who really do not care to be entertained at all. At one end of the scale these people may be polite and unmoved by your magic; at the other end they may be downright rude.

★ Those who are really keen to watch. Some of these will play along, knowing it's all a game but enjoying the attention of everyone around them. In extreme cases, these people can be so taken with you and your skills that they worship the ground you walk on.

★ Those who are interested not so much in your act but in making life hard for you. Some can be very insulting and even physical with their interruptions; others want to play a game of cat and mouse. They just love to think they are one step ahead of you when, of course, it should be the other way around.

This last group is my favourite audience – always a challenge but also your greatest allies once you have convinced them of your skill.

The following card trick, based on a lie detector theme, is very easy to do and will catch out those who think they have one over on you. Through these very simple means you can prove your wonderful powers of Telepathy. I therefore dedicate this trick to all the awkward customers. No matter how hard they try to catch you out, you will always end up ahead of them.

You will need

★ An ordinary deck of cards prepared beforehand for the occasion.

★ An awkward friend.

★ A smattering of magic.

✨ The Trick

One evening, along with a handful of other acquaintances, you are sitting comfortably enjoying a nightcap at your friend Andrew's house. During the evening you have shown the gathering one or two intriguing feats of mind magic which have gone down well. However, Chris has been digging at you, claiming to know what you are doing. You decide the time is right to put him in his place.

'Chris, you seem to know what I am doing all the time, which is very commendable. It's the sign of a good mind-magician in fact. Here, let me show you how easy it is to keep track of someone's thoughts, even yours.'

His back arches: he's spotted the thinly veiled challenge hidden in your compliment. He moves around the table and sits next to you, arms folded.

Taking a deck of cards out of your pocket, you say, 'First I want you to pick a card from this deck.' You spread them between your hands and ask him to take one, look at it and place it back in the deck. You close the cards and place them on the table.

'Some people think that mind-magicians are nothing but liars – would-be criminals who should do something more useful with their time. Well, that may or may not be the case, but it is true that I have to be, let us say, economical with the truth in order to achieve my aims. And you, Chris, seem to know when that is, but I wonder if you are good enough to fool me…

'Chris, I now give you permission to lie at will. I will ask you a few questions and you may answer with truth or fantasy, and I must keep track of your honesty. All I ask is that at the very end, when I ask you to name your card, you answer me truthfully. Is that a deal?' Chris nods in agreement.

'Let us begin. Was your card high or low? A low card you say.' Taking three cards from the top of the deck, you lay them on the table, spelling out the word 'L-O-W' as you do.

'Now, was your card red or black? It was black. OK.' You then lay out five cards, spelling out 'B-L-A-C-K' as you do so.

'Spades or clubs?' You lay down a further five cards as you spell out the reply, 'C-L-U-B-S.'

You now point to the next card. 'Is this your card, Chris?' He shakes his head. 'So what was your card? Be truthful now.' He announces it was the ten of diamonds. 'I can see you have been lying, right to the very end.'

You ask Chris to turn over the card he just denied was his. It is the ten of diamonds. For the rest of the evening Chris seems a little quieter. I wonder why?

✨ Behind the Scenes

There are two secrets to this trick. For the record, neither of them is a force. Your helper has an entirely free choice of card (well, almost). What you must do is to get the chosen card to a specific position, namely fourteenth from the top. You use a craftily marked card for that.

In addition, you use a set of questions that tot up to thirteen or fourteen cards when the answers are spelt out.

Take one card from your deck and put a small pencil mark on the back, along the top edge. Make it just clear enough for you to distinguish that card from the others. Now, with the backs of the cards towards you, place a further twelve cards below it. Place the remainder of the deck on top of this stack of thirteen cards and hold the whole deck in your left hand.

Lean towards your helper and run the cards from your left to your right. Ask him to take one, ensuring that he does so before you get to the marked card. If you do run close to the marked card, close the deck up, look your helper in the eye and remark how useful it would be if he could do it tonight and try again.

Once he has a card in his hand, continue fanning through the deck and comment, 'You could have chosen any one of these. Please look at your card and remember it.' While he looks at his card, take your chance to spot the marked card. Take this card and the twelve below it into your left hand. Offer the cards in your right to your helper and ask him to return his card to the deck. As he places his card on top of the deck, immediately replace the thirteen from your left hand on top.

The chosen card, whatever it is, is now the fourteenth card from the top.

:*: The Performance

If you are unlucky enough not to have an awkward helper for this trick, do not worry. It is played as a challenge, and most people enjoy the thrill of the chase.

Start by having the card chosen as above, then place the deck back on the table face up. This is a psychological ploy, not just to avoid the mark being seen, but also to create the impression that the gathering has seen the whole deck. It sounds crazy, but that will be people's recollection of events.

Now you go into the talk about magicians and liars, all of which creates some very useful misdirection.

Next you get into the questions. There are eight possible combinations of answers, resulting in either the last card dealt, or the next card in the pile being the chosen card.

The table below shows the words you need to spell out, depending upon the answers you get. One point to note is that if you get low and red, you need to spell 'A R-E-D' as there are not enough letters if the response is hearts.

So all you need to do is ask the questions and lead your helper to find his card.

Lie Detector

HIGH/LOW?	RED/BLACK?	SUIT?	YOUR CARD?
HIGH (4)	RED (3)	DIAMOND (7)	POINT TO LAST CARD
HIGH (4)	RED (3)	HEARTS (6)	POINT TO NEXT CARD
HIGH (4)	BLACK (5)	SPADE (5)	POINT TO LAST CARD
HIGH (4)	BLACK (5)	CLUBS (5)	POINT TO LAST CARD
LOW (3)	A RED (4)	DIAMOND (7)	POINT TO LAST CARD
LOW (3)	A RED (4)	HEARTS (6)	POINT TO NEXT CARD
LOW (3)	BLACK (5)	SPADE (5)	POINT TO NEXT CARD
LOW (3)	BLACK (5)	CLUBS (5)	POINT TO NEXT CARD

:*: Final Thoughts

Of course you will need to think on your feet in this trick, but the effect it has on an audience is entertaining. The wise guy will end up in his rightful place – not put there by you so much, but by his friends. Change the patter to suit the situation and the chain of events. For example, if the helper says the last card is theirs, you can say, 'Well, I know for certain you are not lying about that!' and of course you would be right. Try practising a line for each possible outcome.

★ ★ ★ TELECOMMUNICATION ★ ★ ★

In this experiment, the mind- or thought-reading that appears to take place occurs remotely, with a faceless psychic at the other end of a telephone line. More properly, this is an example of clairvoyance and clairaudience – the ability to see and hear over great distances.

You will need

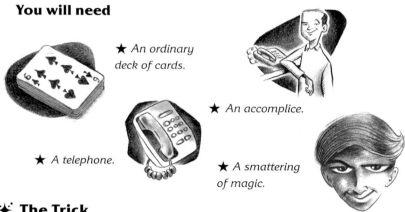

★ An ordinary deck of cards.

★ An accomplice.

★ A telephone.

★ A smattering of magic.

☀ The Trick

You take your cards and play with them modestly while Chris retires to make himself a drink.

'You know, you've seen some interesting feats this evening, and I know you're intrigued by my abilities. But I'm just a novice compared to a friend of mine. He's awesome. Would you like to see what he can do?'

Everyone nods in confirmation.

You instruct Andrew, your host, to take your cards and spread them across the table face up. You explain that you want everyone to see the cards to confirm that they are all present and all different. You then request that Andrew slides one card silently to the side. Let us suppose he chooses the seven of diamonds.

You ask for the telephone: 'I am about to call my friend. I do know his real name but he prefers to be called the Teller.' You dial a number and after a short while the phone at the other end of the line is apparently answered. You ask to speak to the Teller and you tell him you have someone with you who wishes to know something. You hand the phone to Andrew and the conversation goes something like this:

Teller	'Good evening, sir. I am addressing a gentleman, is that correct?'
Andrew	'Er, yes.' He is taken aback that the Teller is aware he is male.
Teller	'My name is the Teller. Who is this, please?'

Andrew	'This is Andrew.'
Teller	'Andrew, you are thinking of a card – is that correct?'
Andrew	'Yes.'
Teller	'I want you to concentrate on an image of your card. Have you done that?'
Andrew	'Yes.'
Teller	'It is a red card, neither low nor high value.'
Andrew	'Yes.'
Teller	'Rather an unusual card for an Aquarian. You are an Aquarian, aren't you?'
Andrew	'Yes.' Again, he is taken aback that the Teller knows his star sign.
Teller	'Your card was the seven of diamonds, is that correct?'
Andrew	'Yes, it was!' Andrew looks confused and somewhat shaken.

The phone call ends. Andrew sits back in his chair, takes a large gulp of his brandy and explains to his guests what happened during the call.

✨ Behind the Scenes

You transmit the information needed by the Teller using a secret code, which is shown in the table below. Study this because you will need to know it well.

When I first used this idea over thirty years ago, it was simply to transmit the name of a playing card. The information about gender and birth sign are more recent additions, which you may choose to leave out for simplicity. You might, of course, wish to be more adventurous and work out ways to transmit other information.

It is also useful to know the birth sign of your helper. You may know it already if they are a friend. You could be bold and ask them or their partner in secret. But the best way is to perform 'Astronome' (see page 51) earlier in the evening and you will have the information you need.

If you don't have a chance to garner this information, do not worry. The effect is powerful anyway. You and your accomplice will both need to be familiar with the code.

The code works in two ways: timing and choice of words. Your audience will probably only ever see this done once, so the subtle differences your conversation with the Teller might take will not be apparent to them.

During your call the Teller will slowly say a number of things, unheard by the audience. You transmit the required information to him by interrupting him at the right moment. Slight variations in your words will also give him other clues.

✦ The Performance

You ask your chosen helper to spread the cards on the table, face up and in a random fashion if possible. This gives you an opportunity to explain that this exercise is to be done as openly and fairly as possible.

Ask the helper to slide a card out. Insist that nothing is said 'in case the room is bugged', but do make a note of the card yourself.

COUNT CARD VALUES	COUNT SUITS	WHO DO YOU HAVE	REQUEST TO THE TELLER	SIGN	ELEMENT	DATES
Ace	Clubs	I have someone here	They are thinking of a card	Libra	Air	Sept 23–Oct 22
2	Hearts		They are thinking of a card	Aquarius	Air	Jan 20–Feb 18
3	Spades	Caller is male	They are thinking of a card	Gemini	Air	May 12–June 20
4			They are thinking of something	Cancer	Water	June 21–July 22
5			They are thinking of something	Scorpio	Water	Oct 23–Nov 21
6		I have some one here	They are thinking of something	Pisces	Water	Feb 19–Mar 20
7		Caller is male	They have chosen a card	Capricorn	Earth	Dec 22–Jan 19
8			They have chosen a card	Taurus	Earth	Apr 20–May 20
9			They have chosen a card	Virgo	Earth	Aug 23–Sep 22
10			They are thinking of something	Aries	Fire	Mar 21–Apr 19
Jack			They are thinking of something	Leo	Fire	July 23–Aug 22
Queen			They are thinking of something	Sagittarius	Fire	Nov 22–Dec 21
King			They wish to know their card			

You take the telephone and call the number of the Teller.

When the phone is answered you say, 'Hello, I would like to speak with the Teller, please.'

This alerts your friend, and he begins to count slowly through from ace to king: 'Ace, two, three, four, five, six, seven…' At this point you say, 'Good evening, Teller.' By doing so you have given him his first clue.

He now recites the playing card suits: 'Clubs, hearts, spades, diamonds,' at which point you say, 'I have someone with me' if it is a man helping you, or 'I have somebody with me' if it is a woman.

You have now given them the suit of the card and the gender of the caller. You continue with one of the following four lines:

1. **'They are thinking of a card'** . . . . *if their birth sign is an air sign.*
2. **'They are thinking of something'** . . . . *if their birth sign is a water sign.*
3. **'They have chosen a card'** . . . . *if their birth sign is an earth sign.*
4. **'They have chosen something'** . . . . . . *if their birth sign is a fire sign.*

Now the Teller must say the three names within the sign type (air, water, fire or earth). Aquarius is an air sign, so they will say 'Gemini, Libra, Aquarius…' at which point you say, 'I will hand them to you now.'

If you have not been able to establish your helper's birth sign, you need to let the Teller know, so say, 'They wish to know their card' instead.

Hand the phone to your helper, and ask them not to say anything until the Teller has spoken (this prevents them from saying hello, which lessens the impact of guessing the gender).

✦ Final Thoughts

As there are several things to remember with this trick, I have prepared a small table to guide you. You will need to become familiar with the table and perhaps ask the Teller to keep a copy near his phone.

It's most important that as you talk with the Teller there are no awkward pauses and that you speak with confidence and pace. It would be easy to do this badly and give the game away.

The choice of Teller is important. You must be able to rely on your accomplice, and he or she in turn must be able to speak clearly and confidently to your helper.

Oh, and finally, it would be better if your helper does not know the friend playing the Teller. The impact would be lost if Andrew were to stop halfway through and say, 'Marian, that's you, isn't it?'

★ ★ ★ ONE HEAD IS BETTER ★ ★ ★ ★

So you have shown the assembled audience your ability to read thoughts and transfer them over long distances. Now you're going to do something that will really stun them: read three minds in quick succession.

This particular trick is a very useful one to have in your repertoire because it can be performed totally impromptu and once again demonstrates your wonderful powers of telepathy. It also teaches you about a very important principle in mind magic, more of which later.

You will need

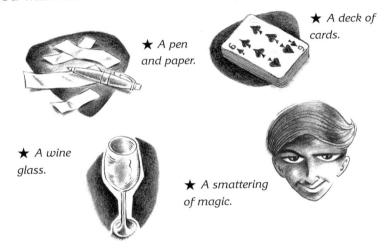

★ A deck of cards.

★ A pen and paper.

★ A wine glass.

★ A smattering of magic.

✴ The Trick

Andrew's guests have gathered around him to find out what happened during his conversation with the Teller.

'I did tell you he was awesome,' you remark, and Andrew nods in agreement.

'In fact, he and I often set each other little challenges. An occasional competition to see who can perform the best feats of mind magic. All in the name of enhancing the science, of course,' you say, giving a wry smile. 'So I would like to try something particularly challenging – reading minds rapidly one after the other.'

You ask for a pen and some slips of paper, a deck of cards and a wine glass. You hand the cards to Andrew to shuffle and take them back.

'Very good. We shall start with reading number one.' As you speak you write the number in the corner of a slip of paper.

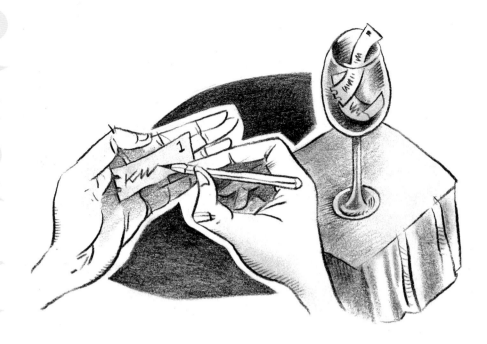

'Joshua, I want you to think of anyone present here this evening. Do not tell me or anyone else who it is. Just concentrate on the name for a moment.'

You pause and look at Joshua with a firm gaze. 'OK, I have the name.' You write the name on the paper, fold it and place it in the wine glass, which you give to Andrew for safe-keeping.

'Joshua, we will now ask something of your chosen person for reading number two.' You write the number in the corner of a new slip of paper. 'Who were you thinking of? Emma? Very well, Emma, will you please think of any date in history?' Again a firm, emotionless gaze as you read Emma's thoughts. 'That's excellent.' You write down what you have received, fold the slip and place it in the wine glass held by Andrew. 'May I ask what date you thought of? 16 July 1986.' She adds that it was her wedding day.

You pick up the cards and say, 'Now for our third reading we need an entirely random thought. Daniel, would you be so kind as to choose a card? We will leave that card unknown for now: please just touch the deck with your right hand and concentrate on the cards for me.' You write down the number 3 and the name of the card you received on a final slip of paper, fold it and put it with the others in the wine glass.

Now you turn to Andrew: 'I would like you to take the slips of paper out of the glass. Do not read aloud what they say yet. Simply get them in order – 1, 2, 3.'

Once Andrew has sorted the papers, you turn to Joshua: 'I asked you to think of anyone present. You said Emma. Andrew, what is written on the first slip?' He confirms it shows EMMA.

'Now, Emma, I asked you to think of any date: you said 16 July 1986. What does the slip say?' Andrew again confirms you are correct.

'Now the one fact no one knows, not even Daniel, is his chosen card. Andrew what did I write, please?' He tells everyone you wrote the four of hearts. 'Daniel, will you now show us the card you chose?' He slowly turns it over for all to see. It is the four of hearts.

You pull on your coat and leave quietly. You will be invited back soon.

✳ Behind the Scenes

By now you will have guessed that knowing the card was established by using the cross-cut force described earlier (see page 14). But how could you know the other thoughts? Quite simply you got your helpers to tell you – right out loud.

This trick uses a nifty idea known as the 'one-ahead principle'. Just by knowing one of the three thoughts in advance and by blatantly lying about what you are actually writing on the slips you can appear to read minds.

What is really sneaky is how you get to know which card to force after they have been shuffled. In fact, when you take the cards back from your volunteer shuffler you see the card you want to force on the bottom of the deck. This, however, is entirely the wrong place. You want it on the top.

If you can shuffle cards with a regular overhand shuffle, you can easily move the bottom card to the top. Holding the cards in your left hand with their backs towards you, remove about half the cards from the bottom of the deck with your right hand. The card to be forced is now on the bottom of the cards in your right hand.

Shuffle the cards in your right hand on to the ones in your left a few at a time. As you get towards the last cards in your right hand, drag them off one at a time into your left hand, making sure the bottom card goes on last. You are now set for the force.

The next stage involves the one-ahead principle, which calls for a lot of bare-faced cheek, but that, after all, is an important gift for a mind-magician.

When you wrote down Joshua's choice of Emma on slip one, you lied. In fact, you wrote out slip three, naming the card.

When you wrote Emma's date on slip two, you also lied. You, in fact, completed slip one with her name – after all, you knew it because Joshua had told you.

Finally, you didn't write out the name of the card on slip three. Instead, you wrote the chosen date on slip two. Cheeky but deceptive and very effective!

☀ The Performance

There is a lot to learn in this trick, and it's important to get things in just the right order.

Gather everyone around and assemble all the props you need. Hand over the cards to be shuffled. Take them back but get a glimpse and make a mental note of the bottom card. This is the one you will be forcing later.

Explain how you will read three minds in quick succession, pick up a slip of paper and pretend to start your first reading. Write a number 3 in the top corner of the slip, saying aloud, 'Number 1,' as you do so. Ask your first helper to think of someone present, play-act a little as you 'read their mind', then write down the name of the playing card to be forced. Fold the slip into quarters and drop it into the glass. Giving the glass to someone else to hold for you is a good ploy because it clearly shows that you cannot tamper with the written slips.

Now prepare the second slip, saying aloud. 'Number 2,' as you write 1 in the corner. Call for the name of the person chosen and ask them to think of a date. Pause to receive their thoughts, then write the name given earlier on the slip, fold it and place in the glass.

Now pick up the cards and announce that you need a random thought for the final reading, casually shuffling the cards and bringing the bottom card to the top as explained above. As an aside, ask the second helper about the date they chose.

Ask the third helper to cut the cards and leave them crossed, as in the force (see page 14). Write number 2 on the slip and say, 'Finally, number 3.' Ask the helper to touch the cards and transmit a thought to you. You write down the chosen date, then fold and deposit the slip.

Everything is now in place. All that remains is for you to make a dramatic revelation of your amazing mind readings.

☀ Final Thoughts

There you have it – an epic trick by any measure. In fact, there is a classic trick called 'Mental Epic' that uses a similar principle but adds some more complex mechanics to make it work. The beauty of the version described here is that you can perform it almost any time. Just remember the following points when you do so.

1. Make sure when you do the false shuffle to keep the card backs uppermost. This prevents the chosen card from being spotted earlier by a sharp-eyed spectator.

2. Use your words carefully when asking the keeper of the glass to read out the slips of paper. Make sure he reads them just one at a time and only when you ask.

IS SOMEBODY OUT THERE?

'The distance that the dead have gone
Does not at first appear–
Their coming back seems possible
For many an ardent year.'

EMILY DICKINSON (1830–86)

Where does our spirit go to when our time upon this earth is done? Some believe that death is the end of everything. Others say that the spirit lives on beyond the grave, allowing us to connect with those who have gone before and those who remain behind.

Some believe that the departed are constantly around us and they go as far to seek proof of the various means that spirits choose to make us aware of their presence. These include actually appearing to us, causing something to move mysteriously, or leaving some lasting mark of their visit with us.

Whatever your belief, you can have a little fun with the following tricks, each one showing a different dimension of spiritual contact. At first glance you might say that they are simple parlour tricks, mere diversions. Yet some who witness them will find a new understanding of the world that lies beyond.

★ ★ ★ A FRIEND FROM THE OTHER SIDE ★ ★ ★

Have you ever felt a strange presence beside you, yet there is nobody there? Maybe a shiver runs down your spine. Some people put these occurrences down to purely physical causes such as temperature changes, but there are those who believe them to be evidence of spirits. Wouldn't it be amazing if you could capture a spirit and prove its existence to the world?

Read on, and I shall explain how you can go about catching a spirit in your own hands.

You will need

★ A short note tailored to suit your chosen friend and the situation you will be in.

★ A specially prepared hand- kerchief.

★ A smattering of magic.

✦ The Trick

You have begun to gain a reputation among your friends for your ability to perform wondrous feats of mind magic. Is it any wonder, therefore, that one Saturday evening, as you sit around your dinner table after a fine meal with a few friends, your guests beg you to show them some of your skills?

You ponder for a moment, then remove your handkerchief from your pocket and casually wipe the corner of your mouth.

'I don't really know that I should show you this. You might think I'm treating the spirits disrespectfully, but you would be wrong.'

Your guests are very intrigued now and make some encouraging noises, urging you to show them more.

'Very well. You should be aware that spirits are around us everywhere and are often frustrated by their inability to make themselves known. Perhaps we can encourage one or two of them to play with us this evening…'

You carefully lay your handkerchief out on the table in front of you and fold three corners towards you. 'I want you all to concentrate on the centre of the handkerchief.' Lightly grasp the two corners now nearest to you and begin to murmur, 'Come, spirit, come. Come join us at this festive board.'

After a moment or two the centre of the handkerchief seems to expand, as if something were now hiding underneath it.

'Welcome spirit,' you say, as the centre fills out a little more. 'I am sure this is a friendly spirit. I have felt his presence many times before and I feel he would like us to touch him as proof of his existence.'

You place the palm of your hand on top of the spirit and move it in a circular motion. Your audience can clearly see the shape of the spirit being formed by your hand. You look at Evelyn, who is sitting to your right, and say, 'Here, give me your hand.' Evelyn tentatively allows you to guide her to touch the spirit, then pulls away with a start as she definitely feels the spirit inside.

'Don't worry. He knows many people find his presence a little frightening, and for those of you who doubt what Evelyn felt, I will show you more proof.'

You pick up a spoon from the table and gently tap the top of the spirit with the bowl of the spoon. The banging sound tells everyone that there is clearly something solid under the handkerchief.

'Do we have any more volunteers to touch our friend?' you ask.

There are no takers. 'Very well, I will ask him to leave now.'

Once again, you place your palm on top of the spirit, and as your hand moves slowly in a circular motion, the spirit slowly fades away. You thank him quietly, lifting the handkerchief to show that nothing physical or spiritual is hiding within it – except, that is, for a small, folded slip of paper which has the letter E drawn on the outside. You pick it up and say, 'This is for you, I believe, Evelyn. Will you read out what it says?'

She unfolds the note and reads: 'Evelyn, I did not wish to scare you this evening. My purpose here is simply to let you know of my presence. I assure you that I and any other spirit you may encounter this evening has only good intentions.'

You begin to murmur some more, but you will have to wait a while to find out what and why.

✦ Behind the Scenes

The handkerchief is specially prepared. Quite simply a long match or cocktail stick is inserted into the hem at one of the corners. By correctly folding and manipulating the handkerchief you create the impression of there being something solid inside.

If you prefer, you can use a cloth napkin rather than a handkerchief for this trick. Choose whatever suits you best.

The note to your helper is pre-written by you. If you are certain who your guests will be before they arrive, you can have fun writing something particularly relevant to one of them. Keep the note handy in a pocket or somewhere you can get hold of it easily and quickly. You have to sneak it under the handkerchief during the performance.

This little 'miracle' is perfect after-dinner entertainment, and can be worked more or less anywhere on the dining table with people all around you. Ideally, the table should have a tablecloth on it; it doesn't work so well on a shiny surface. You will also need to practise in order to get the effect looking just right. Key to this is folding the handkerchief correctly, and the diagrams below should help.

Lay the handkerchief out in front of you like a diamond shape, two corners pointing left and right, one pointing towards you, and the corner furthest away from you having the match in the seam. You should arrange it so that the match is to the left of the point.

Fold the match corner (A) down towards you so that it lies about 7.5 cm (3 in) from the corner nearest you (C). Next, fold the right corner (B) on to corner (C).

Now, if you slowly pull the left corner (D) towards the right, the handkerchief will lever itself up slightly on to the match. Experiment with this motion and you will see that the whole hanky seems to fill up, not just the portion around the match. Now,

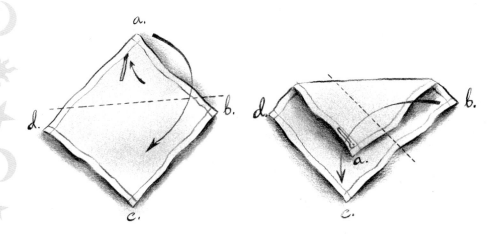

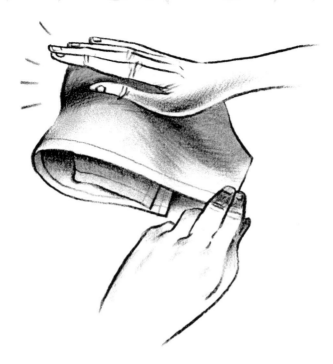

if you place your palm on top of the match, you can move it around like a joystick. Again, the folds will create the impression of movement all over the handkerchief.

Play around with these manoeuvres until you can make them look smooth and thus acheive an eerie effect.

✦ The Performance

It is important to be serious but not over-intense when performing this trick, otherwise you risk making it look like a novelty or joke.

Lay the handkerchief out and fold it as directed. This is best done in silence, as you should give the impression that you are thinking about what you are doing.

When you have finished folding, hold corner B firmly against the tabletop in your left hand. Reach over and take corner D in your right. Make your murmurings in a breathy voice, not too dramatically, and use only normal words. Allow the handkerchief to rise slightly, then bring it up some more. Corner D will pass over the top of B.

Now, with your left hand still on corner B, release your right hand from corner D and place the palm on top of the 'spirit', slowly moving the hand around to show the presence within. Ask your helper to offer you their hand. Grasp it firmly and a little uncomfortably for them, perhaps holding it at a slightly awkward angle. Allow them to touch the match and 'feel the spirit'. If you let go of their hand suddenly and jump a little in your chair, it should make them recoil very smartly.

Using the spoon is quite a startling thing for the audience to witness. If you hit the match right on top, you can do so with quite a lot of force. The louder the knock you can make, the better.

Put the spoon down on the table and allow your hands to fall to your sides. Look around at your guests, gazing directly into their eyes one by one and offer the opportunity to touch the spirit. Some might volunteer, some might not. Whatever happens, this is a good moment to get hold of the note in your left hand. Hold it close to the palm with your thumb and slightly curl your fingers to shield it from view. Practise holding it so that your hand looks natural.

When you are ready to say goodbye to the spirit, gently place your right palm on top of 'him' for the last time. Slowly move your hand around and gradually make the match lower to create the effect that the spirit is drifting away.

Take corner D in your right hand and lift it upwards at the same time that your left hand moves out, grasps corner B and drops the note into the folds. The drop should be screened by the raised handkerchief.

Lift up the hanky by the two corners and turn it about to prove that it's empty. Do not draw attention yet to the note. With luck, one of your guests will pick it up first. In any case, make sure you look surprised by its arrival.

Pace your performance nicely, with dignity and decorum, and you will create a miracle. Play it for laughs and you have nothing but a joke that will spoil your reputation as a mind-magician.

Once you have mastered the movements, you can do more with this trick if you like. You can choose to leave out the note if you are not comfortable with the secret moves to drop it. On the other hand, you might choose to become more adventurous and put something more substantial inside, such as a coin, a ring, a small crystal, or even an item you 'borrowed' earlier.

★ ★ ★ RISE TO THE OCCASION ★ ★ ★

Earlier in the book you saw a ring being moved mysteriously through the power of telekinesis. Now you will witness something far more dramatic: the levitation of a table by angry spirits.

If you play this one as described, it will be very shocking to your guests, as the climax comes quite unexpectedly. If you can enlist the assistance of a secret helper from among your guests, the trick becomes even more effective.

You will need

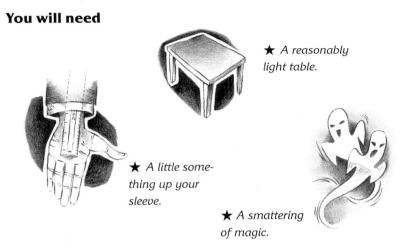

★ A reasonably light table.

★ A little some-thing up your sleeve.

★ A smattering of magic.

✦ The Trick

Returning to our story… After you have sent the friendly spirit back to the other side, you begin to look uncomfortable and start to murmur strange things. The table begins to vibrate slowly, then more and more. 'Oh, my goodness,' you say. 'I think we've woken up another spirit. Quickly, all please stand and place your hands flat on the table.' Your friends do as asked.

The table starts to shake even more violently. One edge rises up, then down. Another edge rises up, then down.

Suddenly, the whole table rises off the ground, perhaps 30 cm (1 ft) or more. 'Help me keep the table down!' you say in a panic. Your friends do their best to help as the table bobs up and down. 'If we can keep the table under control, it will soon pass.'

The table then slowly starts to revolve to the right. You all work to pull it back. It tries once more, you bring it back again. Everyone gasps as it suddenly jolts to the right, taking everyone with it.

You and your guests struggle with the wild spirit controlling the table for what seems like an age, but is in reality perhaps just twenty or thirty seconds. Eventually, the table begins to calm down and slowly sinks back to the floor.

'Good, it has passed,' you say. 'Who would like to see something more?'

✴ Behind the Scenes

Like all good mind magic, the secret of this trick is devilishly simple.

Hidden up each sleeve of your shirt or jacket you have a rod. Each rod, made of wood, metal or plastic, should be about 30 cm (1 ft) long. A sturdy ruler of some kind would be good, or perhaps some dowelling. Have a look around your home and see what you can find.

Whatever you choose to make your rods from, they should be shorter than your forearm, as they will be strapped to you and you do not want to have your movement restricted.

Each rod should be fixed to you by two straps placed around your arm, one close to the wrist and the other about halfway along. The rods should be held firmly but still be free enough for you to slide them in and out with ease.

Draw out the rods so that they are touching the middle of your palms. Place your hands near the edge of the table so that the rods go beneath it, then rest your hands flat on the table. If you now flex your wrists upwards, the table will be gripped between your hands and the rods. By moving your arms up, down and from side to side, you can make the table move mysteriously.

Experiment with the rods and a suitable table until you have mastered the art of flotation.

If you have a friend you can trust implicitly, you might want to let them in on the secret. With two people, each controlling opposite sides of the table, the motion will become much greater, a lot smoother and more realistic.

✳ The Performance

The attraction of this trick lies not just in the shock value when you suddenly become concerned, but also in the way you railroad your audience into helping you.

Sometime prior to your performance, make your excuses and go to the bathroom. Fit your rods, then return to continue entertaining your guests. If you have a secret helper, it is best that he or she visits the bathroom a decent interval before or after you, to avoid arousing suspicion.

While your guests are still musing over the previous trick, secretly reach into your sleeves and pull forward your rods. Slip them under the table and choose your moment to begin.

Start off slowly, expressing concern about what is happening. Make the table shudder by moving your hands. It does not matter that your hands are seen to move because they are, of course, touching the table and would move anyway.

Gradually make the movements more pronounced. Show more concern and speak a little more frantically. Ask everyone to stand and put their hands on the table, at which point you can make the table begin to rise and fall.

Move your hands to the right, but not your body. The table will move rightwards, so now follow with your body. Make it look as if the table suddenly pulled you along.

Keep up the movements for thirty seconds or so, moving from side to side and up and down. Gradually become a little calmer as you get things 'under control' and let the table come to a rest.

As you withdraw your hands, casually bend your fingers and push the rods back up into your sleeves.

✳ Final Thoughts

Surprise is the key to this trick, so why not think about doing it elsewhere? Tables in cafés and coffee shops tend to be fairly small and light, so you could do it unaided very easily and effectively.

Choose your moment, but pretend to go into a sort of trance and make the table rise. The café manager will either love it and want you to show more of your mind magic, or throw you out before you have even paid for your coffee...

★ ★ ★ THE MARK OF THE POLTERGEIST ★ ★ ★

One of the very first tricks I learned as a young boy was a weird exercise showing the power of voodoo. While easy to do, it was both powerful and shocking to my chosen helper. It involved the mysterious appearance of some cigarette ash on the palm of their hand.

I still perform this trick in its original form from time to time. However, since smoking has become less popular and acceptable, I have devised the alternative version below. Once again, given the right time and place, this trick can be extremely effective.

You will need

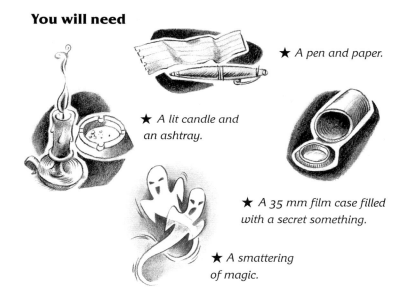

★ A pen and paper.

★ A lit candle and an ashtray.

★ A 35 mm film case filled with a secret something.

★ A smattering of magic.

✳ The Trick

Your dinner guests have become more than a little excited by their encounter with the angry spirit who controlled the table. 'I think we should slow down a little, to calm our souls,' you say, as you walk over to the mantelpiece and pick up the candlestick holding a candle that has been burning all evening.

'I am not surprised that we encountered that spirit. I have been aware for some time that a lost soul exists here.' You carry the candlestick over to the table, put it down and take your seat once more.

'Let me tell you what I know. This house was built around 105 years ago, and when I bought it last year I took the time to research its history. For the last twenty

years or so it belonged to the Hawkins family and was simply a family home. Before that it was a general grocery shop. I am not sure how long it had been a shop but I do know that the first owner shared much in common with me.'

Your guests watch intently as the light from the candle flickers in your eyes. 'Dr Marcus was also deeply intrigued by the paranormal and carried out experiments such as I do. He even wrote a book once, a book I would dearly love to read. Sadly, there are not many copies surviving.

'Dr Marcus himself died in mysterious circumstances in a fire in this very room. Nobody knows for certain how or why the fire started. All I know is that his spirit is around us and that he was not a man who would wish to harm us. I am sure he too just wishes to let us know he is here. Perhaps we should see if he will give us a sign.'

You take out a slip of paper, write on it 'Dr Marcus – Requiescat in Pace', fold it up and place it in the ashtray.

'Now I would like you all to help me. Make your right hand into a lightly clenched fist and hold it to your heart. Here – I'll show you how.'

You take hold of Peter's hand, close it into a fist and direct him to hold it to his chest. You see that Adam and Toby also need some help, you assist them in the same way.

You take the slip of paper in your right hand and hold it to the candle so that it catches alight. 'Dr Marcus, if you can hear me, I want you to send us a sign. We have felt you around us this evening and we wish you nothing but peace. Please leave a sign with one of the mortal souls here in your home, a sign to say you hear us.'

You turn and angle the note as it burns through, eventually dropping it into the ashtray when the flames come too close to your fingers. You remain silent for a moment and watch the flame die away as you pinch a small amount of ash with your right hand fingers and rub it into your left palm. 'This will be the sign,' you announce.

'Please, one at a time, open your hands to see if Dr Marcus has left a message with you.'

You point to each of your guests in turn. Adam opens his hand: he has nothing. Toby looks at his hand: it is also empty, and so is Evelyn's.

'Peter, before you open your hand, may I ask, did you feel anything during our little ritual just now?' Peter seems unsure – maybe, maybe not.

'Open your hand now, Peter.' As he slowly unclenches his fist, he turns pale. There, in the centre of his palm, is a dab of black ash.

'Peter, it seems the sign has been left with you, but do not be perturbed. Simply be aware that this evening you have had the honour of communicating with a spirit, something most mortal men never experience.'

✦ Behind the Scenes

This trick makes use of our old friend, misdirection. In this particular case, time is used to create misdirection. You secretly put the ash mark on your unwitting helper's palm right at the beginning of the ritual, when you showed them how to hold their hand.

So much time and action passes between that moment and the point when the hand is opened that most people will have completely forgotten that you went anywhere near their hands.

To prepare for this trick you should half-fill your film case with ash from some paper you have burned previously.

Pick a trustworthy volunteer to practise with. Dip the index finger of your right hand in the case so that you have a good amount of ash on it. Go through the action of taking your helper's right hand (as in the diagram on the left) and guiding it towards their chest. As you withdraw your hand, your index finger can easily deposit the ash in their palm with a simple rub. You then help them to clench their hand into a fist and continue to guide it until it is resting on their heart.

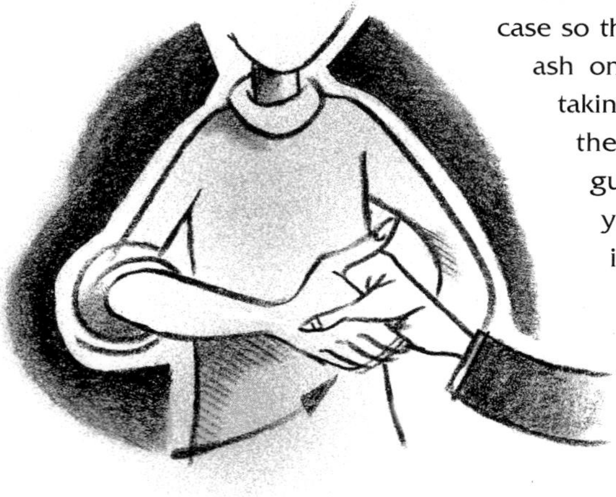

✳ The Performance

Prior to performing, place the lid on the film case and put it safely in your jacket pocket. If you have a ticket pocket inside your main pocket, you could use that to hold the case. Also put the pen and paper you are going to use in the same pocket.

When you are getting close to your chosen moment, casually put your hand in your pocket and flip the lid off the film case. You are now all set.

Begin your story, and at the appropriate moment go to your pocket and take out the pen and paper. Write the name of your deceased person on the slip, fold it and place it in the ashtray. Now put the pen back in your pocket, pushing your finger into the film case to coat it with ash.

Ask your guests to clench their fists and hold them to their heart. Without pausing, take one person's hand and show exactly what you want. At the same time, of course, leave the ash mark in their palm. Try to help one or two others as well to deflect attention from your chosen 'victim'.

Now everything is ready, you can enjoy making the little ritual and building the suspense. Ask for the hands to be opened one at a time, leaving the marked one till last.

✳ Final Thoughts

In this chapter we have dealt with some sensitive material. Most people are wary of things to do with spirits, so it is important to accompany the tricks with positive messages. The spirits are not here to harm us – they just want to exist alongside us.

The appearance of ash in the hand can hit people quite dramatically, especially when their senses are dulled with alcohol. So do try to find some good reasoning behind the experience, perhaps remarking that it is a rare honour, as suggested to Peter in the story above.

WRITTEN IN THE STARS

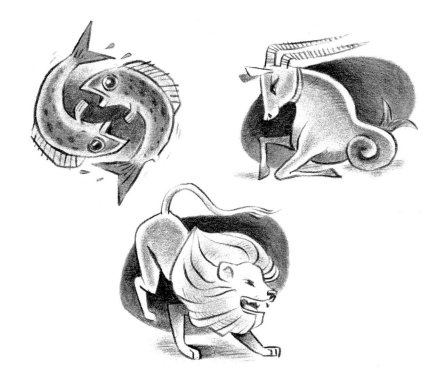

'We need not feel ashamed of flirting with the zodiac. The zodiac is
well worth flirting with.'

D. H. Lawrence (1885-1930)

Human beings seem to have devised myriad ways to interpret their inner selves
and predict the future. From palms to pendulums and tarot to tea, it seems almost
anything that appears to behave or react randomly has been used by seers and
psychics. Some of the more amusing techniques include divination using horses,
cats and itches, while cromniomancy tells fortunes using onions.

This chapter looks at some popular forms of fortune-telling, using a little mind magic
to help you on your way. You will also learn something of an ancient tool that has been
used for centuries by those wishing to give the impression they have 'special powers'.

★ ★ ★ ★ ASTRONOME ★ ★ ★ ★

Most of us will be familiar with Astrology to some degree or other. We simply cannot escape the daily columns of advice freely given to us in newspapers and magazines. This is a diverting trick that involves both astrology and mind magic – an irresistible combination for most audiences.

You will need

★ *A set of twelve cards, numbered from one to twelve on one side and bearing a sign of the zodiac on the other.*

★ *A prediction card in an envelope.*

★ *A smattering of magic.*

☀ The Trick

It is a cold mid-week afternoon, and you are sitting quietly at home expecting a visitor. The doorbell rings, so you open the door and greet Susan. She is a new acquaintance, a girlfriend of your brother John. Susan has been staying near your home on business, and you have invited her round for coffee.

The conversation ranges over many subjects and inevitably turns to your unusual abilities.

'You know, Susan, many people are avid readers of the daily horoscopes found in the popular press. I'm not sure whether these can be truly personal enough to have any real meaning, but I am certain that astrology can tell us much about ourselves in relation to the world and those around us.'

You begin to lay out some cards on the table in front of you. There are twelve, numbered one to twelve, and you lay them out in a circle, as a clock face. In the centre of the circle you place a small envelope. 'This is something I prepared for you a little earlier.

'Susan, many people have a number that is special or lucky to them. Usually it's a small number. Do you have such a lucky number?'

Susan nods.

'And can you see it on one of these cards?'

Again she nods.

'Now in a moment I want you to spell that number out in your mind, counting around the circle as you do so. One card for each letter, starting of course at number one. I will turn my back so I cannot see what you are doing.'

Susan counts around the circle and indicates when she has finished.

'Good. Now I want you to note the number you have landed on and spell that number out in the same way, starting with the card after it.'

Once again she counts and tells you when she has finished.

'Now, for the third time, please repeat the process, spelling the number of the card you are on right now and continuing to count round the circle. When you are done I want you to take the card you have stopped on and lay it on top of the envelope.'

When she has finished, you turn back towards her and ask her to reverse the remaining eleven cards, each one showing a different sign of the zodiac on it.

'Now please turn over the card you have chosen. What sign is on that card? Pisces... Does that have any meaning for you, Susan?' She looks a little confused, so you direct her to open the envelope and read the short note inside: 'Dear Susan, today your free and independent thought of a number has led you to a choose single star sign – Pisces.'

She looks somewhat amazed that you knew where she would end up.

'I'm glad you have found your way to this sign. I feel sure this is a good omen for you, perhaps indicating a strong connection with somebody born under the sign of Pisces, such as John, who was born on March 18.'

A warm glow comes to Susan's face and she asks to be shown some more mind magic.

✳ Behind the Scenes

This trick demonstrates an interesting mathematical curiosity. As long as a simple set of instructions is followed, it is possible to ensure exactly which number your helper will eventually finish on.

You may have gathered by now that this is another example of forcing – an apparently free choice that is actually pre-determined by the mind-magician.

In order to prove the theory behind this trick, I suggest you take a piece of paper and draw a circle, placing the numbers one to twelve around the outside, as on a clock face.

Now select a number – let's say five. Starting at one, spell the word 'five', moving one number for each letter, F-1, I-2, V-3, E-4. You stop on number four, so starting at the next number, spell 'four': F-5, O-6, U-7, R-8. Now you are at number eight, so spell 'eight': E-9, I-10, G-11, H-12, T-1. This brings you back to where you started.

SIGN	SYMBOL	DATES	ELEMENT	RULING PLANET
Aries	Ram	March 21–April 19	Fire	Mars
Taurus	Bull	April 20–May 20	Earth	Venus
Gemini	Twins	May 21–June 20	Air	Mercury
Cancer	Crab	June 21–July 22	Water	Moon
Leo	Lion	July 23–Aug 22	Fire	Sun
Virgo	Virgin	Aug 23–Sept 22	Earth	Mercury
Libra	Scales	Sept 23–Oct 22	Air	Venus
Scorpio	Scorpion	Oct 23–Nov 21	Water	Mars/Pluto
Sagittarius	Archer	Nov 22–Dec 21	Fire	Jupiter
Capricorn	Sea Goat	Dec 22–Jan 19	Earth	Saturn
Aquarius	Water Bearer	Jan 20–Feb 18	Air	Saturn/Uranus
Pisces	Fish	Feb 19–March 20	Water	Jupiter/Neptune

Try it again a few times. Start by choosing any number from one to twelve. You will see how you always end up at number one.

You can use this clever little force to make your helper pick almost any piece of information you chose to 'predict' within your envelope. However, as this trick is based upon astrology, it would be useful if you were to have a little knowledge of the subject. I have therefore prepared a simple table of sun signs and their relevant dates, plus some other useful information that can be used to make you appear more knowledgeable.

✳ The Performance

Prepare your zodiac cards with symbols on one side and the numbers from one to twelve on the other. There is no specific order in which they need to be numbered, but you should draw the symbol for your target sign on card number one.

Draft a short note relevant to the person you will be performing for and place it in an envelope. If you can establish the person's sign, or that of their partner, without them knowing, all the better. You can then appear to have even greater gifts.

Carefully arrange the cards in a circle on the table. Take care not to show the undersides that bear the zodiac signs. Revealing them won't exactly ruin the effect, but may set up some expectation of what is going to happen. This can sometimes lessen the impact.

Ensure the cards are conveniently placed for your helper to count around. You want to make it comfortable so that no errors are made, causing you to end up at the wrong number.

Take your helper through the counting instructions slowly and carefully, trying to follow the script above as closely as possible. When they arrive back at number one, instruct them to turn over all the cards except the one they have arrived at. Finally, match their chosen card with your prediction.

✳ Final Thoughts

You should pay particular attention to the words used in this trick. First, any errors in the counting will make things very tricky for you, but second, and more importantly, there are some key lessons about mind magic in this story.

Following the counting, I did not tell Susan to look at the card she had 'ended up on' or 'landed on' or even 'arrived at', for that implies it was not in her control. What I suggested to Susan was that she had 'chosen' that particular card and thus 'chosen' the sign Pisces. As a result, when she comes to recount this story in the future, she will clearly remember that it was a free and unforced choice.

★ ★ ★ THE MYSTICAL TAROT ★ ★ ★ ★

The exact origins of tarot cards are lost in the mists of time. However, it is known that the word 'tarot' is derived from the Hebrew word *torah*, which is the first five books of the ancient Bible.

The tarot deck is split into two halves. The major arcana has twenty-two cards depicting a journey from birth to enlightenment, with one card for each letter of the Hebrew alphabet. The minor arcana consists of fifty-six cards and bears a very close relationship to the standard Western deck of fifty-two cards.

The study of tarot is most absorbing, and I could write a whole book on that subject alone, but for now we will concentrate on a simple but effective trick with just the major arcana.

You will need

★ *A stick of glue.*

★ *The twenty-two cards of the major arcana.*

★ *A sheet showing the meanings of the cards.*

★ *A smattering of magic.*

✳ The Trick

Susan is still with you in your home and seems set on staying until you tell her more.

'I wonder, Susan, have you ever had a tarot card reading? You haven't? Well, it can be most revealing, but sadly we don't have time for a full reading. However, I would like to use my tarot cards to make a small prediction for you.'

You go to a drawer and remove a set of cards. You keep your back to Susan, but she is aware that you are looking through the cards.

'Ah yes, that will do,' you remark, and you bring the cards to the table wrapped in a silk cloth. You also have a sheet of paper, which you place in front of Susan.

'I am sure you know that every tarot card has a unique meaning. This list shows the meaning for the twenty-two most important cards. I would like you to take your time and read the definitions. When you have found the one that is most applicable to you at this moment in time, please let me know which it is.'

Susan peruses the list for a few minutes. After a short while she announces that the Death card is like her because she feels that it is hard to move forward in life.

'What an unbelievable coincidence!' you say. 'Or maybe there was more here than at first meet the eye.'

You open the silk cloth, take out your tarot cards and spread them out slowly between your hands. One card in the spread is seen to be reversed, with its back facing outwards. You slowly withdraw the card: it is number thirteen – Death.

'I am not surprised that card was reversed, for every tarot card has two meanings. A first one and a second, for when the card is itself reversed during a reading. So these cards truly know of your life. Would you like to know more?'

Susan is astounded by this turn of events. Of course, she wishes to know more…

✴ Behind the Scenes

In the previous trick we used a force to control Susan's choice. In this one, however, she truly does have a free choice. The twenty-two tarot cards are cleverly gimmicked, so you can make any card appear reversed from the rest of the deck.

First separate the odd-numbered cards and the even-numbered cards (the Fool, card 0, counts as an even card). Along the top edge of the backs of the odd cards place a very fine smear of stick glue. Now arrange the cards into pairs, one odd and one even, stuck back to back. Place card one against card two and so on. Now arrange all the pairs so that the even numbers are all facing the same way.

If you spread or fan the cards between your hands, you will see that the pairs stick together, so the backs will not show. However, if you apply direct pressure on a pair of cards, they will easily separate, showing one card reversed.

Of course, you also need a list of tarot meanings, so I have prepared brief definitions for each card, one of which is the reverse meaning.

TAROT MEANINGS

0 – THE FOOL: You are facing a crucial decision in your life. Great caution is advised. In reverse: Those around you feel that you are considering the wrong path.

I – THE SORCERER: You have the power and will to achieve. You crave accomplishment. In reverse: You feel unable or too weak to pursue your goals.

II – THE HIGH PRIESTESS: Although you do not always show it, you are a spiritual person not driven by materialism. In reverse: You often find yourself swayed by material possessions.

III – THE EMPRESS: You are a natural parent, yet you are sometimes hampered by vanity and selfish thoughts. In reverse: You lack specific goals and seek to experience life as it unravels.

IV – THE EMPEROR: You feel strong and wise, able to stand your ground. In reverse: You feel the need to receive much help from those in authority.

V – THE HIGH PRIEST: You have great concern for matters of the spirit and seek to avoid the dogma of religion. In reverse: You have a rebellious nature, fighting against social norms or standards imposed by others.

VI – THE LOVERS: You have a love of beauty and have made hasty decisions in love. In reverse: You are experiencing conflicts in love or marriage.

VII – THE CHARIOT: There is much happening around you at a pace you find hard to follow. In reverse: You find it hard to control those over whom you should have some influence.

VIII – STRENGTH: You have the strength to share and trust in others. In reverse: You tend to be indecisive and show a lack of will.

IX – THE HERMIT: You believe you are worldly wise but may tend to live in the past. In reverse: You often feel that others are working against you.

X – THE WHEEL OF FORTUNE: You are experiencing positive changes at present. In reverse: You are currently experiencing a trying time.

XI – JUSTICE: You are a firm believer in justice and the law. In reverse: You find it hard to exist within a set of rules or regulations.

XII – THE HANGED MAN: You feel trapped in a period of limbo. In reverse: You seem too concerned with unimportant things.

XIII – DEATH: You feel you are in a period of great change. In reverse: You have given up hope of moving forward.

XIV – TEMPERANCE: You feel happier around harmony and tranquillity. In reverse: You often find yourself over-indulging in life.

XV – THE DEVIL: You feel your natural attractiveness is a great asset. In reverse: You often feel vulnerable to animal urges.

XVI – THE TOWER: You feel at risk of losing important things in life. In reverse: You fear a loved one will lose or suffer greatly.

XVII – THE STAR: You feel you have much more to learn of yourself. In reverse: You fear your arrogance may cause you to lose friends.

XVIII – THE MOON: You are hampered by self-doubt and fears. In reverse: You seek to know what the future holds.

XIX – THE SUN: You often find success or wealth comes to you naturally. In reverse: You feel you must work for every opportunity.

XX – JUDGEMENT: You are waiting for a crucial decision to be made. In reverse: You feel disillusioned.

XXI – THE WORLD: You anticipate travel or promotion in the near future. In reverse: You feel no one is aware of what you have to offer.

✦ The Performance

Your tarot cards should be hidden away in a drawer before you start, and wrapped in a silk cloth or handkerchief, or perhaps held in a small box.

Announce that you will use your cards to make a prediction and retrieve the cards from their place of storage. Play-act a little to give the impression that you are mulling over the cards and selecting one for your prediction. Hand your helper the list and ask them choose the card meaning that seems most appropriate to them.

Once they have announced their choice, you unwrap or open your cards, taking care to expose only one side – the opposite side to the one with their card on it. As Susan chose card thirteen, you opened the cards showing the even side, then spread them to find the corresponding even card (number fourteen). By putting extra pressure on the cards, you will be able to separate the even and odd card, thus exposing the back of the chosen card.

✦ Final Thoughts

This trick does take a little practice and some time to set up. If delivered with compassion and dignity rather than a clever 'Look at me – I found your card', it will have a deep impact on your audience.

★ ★ ★ ★ MY SIXTH SENSE WORTH ★ ★ ★ ★

I am sure that either you or someone you know has at one time allowed curiosity to get the upper hand and visited a fortune-teller. Perhaps at a fair or carnival you decided to hand over your money and disappear into a tent.

More often than not, those who visit fortune-tellers come out feeling at least a little impressed by the amount they have been told. Some will even say, 'She seemed to know everything about me.'

Whatever you choose to believe about psychics and fortune-tellers, there are certainly many who simply wish to cash in on our never-ending curiosity. Whether they read cards, crystal balls or palms, many of them work to a formula that has been handed down for centuries and that always seems to give an accurate reading. What is of more concern, perhaps, is that many of them don't realize it is a script at all, preferring to believe their soothsaying is a gift from their grandmother.

In this trick, you will learn such a script and a very brief lesson in palmistry.

You will need

★ Some wonderful words of wisdom.

★ A little knowledge of the human palm.

★ A smattering of magic.

☀ The Trick

You pour a final cup of coffee for Susan and yourself. You take her right hand in yours, palm upwards and begin.

'Susan, I have very much enjoyed our meeting today and I hope you have too.' She smiles warmly. 'Sadly, I must shortly prepare for an appointment I have this evening, but before we part I want to share some insight with you.

'During our brief meeting, I have attempted to understand you as much as possible, and I offer this interpretation of who you are and where you stand in life. All I ask is that you see what you think fits your story and use it as you will, but do be honest with yourself so that you may challenge and reassure yourself about your perceptions and decisions in the future.'

You point your finger and slowly draw it along her heart line.

'See how this line, your heart line, is longer than this one, your head line? This suggests that your heart perhaps rules your head.

'Your basic honesty has been getting in the way of your progress, so I urge you to look deeply and openly into yourself and your conscience as you digest this reading. Do not let naivety govern your decisions – and do not view everything that happens as bad luck. You control more than you believe you do right now.

'Life is a tricky path, and luck is a function of our own being. Self-honesty and self-esteem are essential to making good choices about life and working with those you meet day to day.

'I know you occasionally feel that your dreams and aspirations are unrealistic. This is because you have sometimes lost faith in others – and with yourself. Let me explain. You see, while at times you can be extroverted, friendly and quite sociable, you frequently feel introverted, wary and a little reserved. Your experience is that it can be unwise to be too honest in revealing yourself to others, and sometimes hide behind false barriers to avoid real contact. Is this perhaps because those close to you have taken advantage of you?

'The strength of your head line tells me you are an independent thinker and that this is very important for you. You don't accept others' opinions without satisfactory proof, unless it's from someone you respect, such as a lawyer or doctor. You prefer a certain amount of change and variety in your life, and become dissatisfied when hemmed in by the restrictions and limitations of life and work. You thrive on creative and original thoughts.

'There have been times in the last year or so when you have had serious doubts as to whether you have made the right decision or done the right thing. Strong and controlled on the outside, you tend to be anxious and insecure on the inside. As a result, many opportunities offered to you in the past have fallen aside because you refuse to take advantage of others, which is a good quality but also a weakness if you let it rule your decisions. This I can tell from the small breaks in your life line.

'Excuse my frankness, but I feel your emotional adjustment has in the past presented some problems for you and your relationships, which is shown by this curve in your heart line. And while you have some personality weaknesses, you are generally able to compensate for them, which is a great strength.

'You have a great deal of unused capacity, which you have not turned to your advantage. You have no need to be over-critical of yourself, but you have let this prevent you from feeling good about your decisions in the past.

'You have a strong need for other people to like and admire you, so you constantly look for ways to improve yourself. I feel you like to read books and articles or do something academic to improve your mind. You have an infinite capacity for understanding people's problems, and you can sympathize with them. But I get the feeling you are firm when confronted with blatant obstinacy or outright stupidity.

'Moving forward, I see you need to be more honest with yourself about your strengths and your minor weaknesses, and use this new insight to realize your potential. I also believe you may be experiencing problems balancing life issues. Feeling good is essential.

'Most importantly, also think of yourself, Susan, because I know you haven't always done so in the past.'

Warmed by the accuracy of your reading, Susan slips off into the cold evening in the knowledge that she has inner strength and much to give.

☀ Behind the Scenes

Mentalists and psychologists know this process as cold reading. It is also known as the 'Barnum Effect', after the famous circus entrepreneur P. T. Barnum.

It is a collection of generalized statements that seem to have personal relevance to us all. This is because they touch on all our basic needs to be accepted and loved, and on the basic human insecurities we all share.

As part of a self awareness training programme, I often use this for large groups of people, perhaps forty at a time, where I ask them to complete a questionnaire (which I subsequently ignore) and return a copy of the script as a reading. Of course, they all think they are getting a unique reading from me.

I then test out the accuracy of my 'insights'. No one ever feels 'This is simply not me at all.' Everyone finds it at least 60 per cent accurate, and most find it over 80 per cent accurate. Many are so intrigued that they refuse to accept it's a ploy on my part.

There is not much to say about the method that is not already written in the script above. Using a palm reading, or perhaps another tool such as cards, is a good way of gaining credibility. After all it is not *me* telling you what I have seen – it is written in your palm.

For reference, the simple map of the palm, left, shows the three major lines you might want to talk about: the heart line (A), the head line (B) and the life line (C).

In general terms, if the heart line is longer than the head line, you might say that someone makes decisions led by the heart. You can say the reverse if the head line is longer. Breaks in the lines imply issues and barriers to success, and curves sometimes imply longer-term or past problems.

The heart line indicates emotional make-up, your need for love and your ability to give love.

The head line reveals intellectual faculties. It indicates your degree of intelligence and concentration. Also it shows your capacity for intuition and emotional judgement.

The life line indicates health, stamina and the condition of the nervous system. It also reveals your enthusiasm for life, your willingness to take on challenges, your self-control and ability to concentrate, as well as the impact of external forces, such as family, health concerns and interpersonal conflicts.

✴ The Performance

When delivering the script, do so with pace and integrity. You are not trying to prove you are a wise guy, simply that you have empathy and understanding for your friend.

Perhaps the most challenging part of this trick is learning the script. The good news is that you need not be word perfect: some parts can even be left out (by accident or design) with no loss of credibility.

If you have difficulty in recalling your script, you could write it out and have it to hand during the reading: 'I have prepared this for you,' and read from the text. You could, of course, allow your subject to take the script home as a memento.

✴ Final Thoughts

With all three tricks in this chapter you must take care not to give the impression that you can predict the future and thus give people life-changing advice. What you can appear to have is a deeper than normal understanding of human nature, which, to an extent, is true, given the nature of cold reading.

Use these readings as a way to intrigue your audience and leave them wanting more of your wonderful mind magic.

MIND CONTROL

'The highest possible stage in moral culture is when we recognize that we ought to control our thoughts.'

CHARLES DARWIN (1809–82)

Most of the mind magic described so far involves the transfer of thoughts from your helpers to you, or the summoning of forces unknown. Sooner or later, however, it will cross your mind that you ought to be able to send thoughts to others. Rather than reading what others are thinking, why not determine or take control their thoughts in some way? If you could do that, surely the next stage is to control of their actions?

History has many examples of this from political propaganda to the advertising we see all around us. The fact is human beings are very easily led. Just as water and electricity always follow the path of least resistance, it seems we do, too.

This fact has been known for centuries, around 350BC the Greek philosopher Demosthenes said 'What we wish... is what we readily believe'. Or put another way, we tend to follow our hearts, not our heads.

So can we use this knowledge to our advantage in performing our Mind Magic? We most certainly can, and magicians have done so since time began.

This chapter therefore presents you with techniques of mind control, and you shall see how easy it is to leave strong men disabled and unable to think, make decisions or act independently.

★ ★ ★ GRIPPING STUFF ★ ★ ★

The human mind is a wonderful thing, capable of every feat imaginable and many yet to be imagined. Yet despite millennia of practice, human beings still let the mind get the better of them from time to time.

This little trick can be quite fun, as someone within a group of people will always react just the way you want.

You will need

★ *A smattering of magic.*

★ *A group of friends.*

✳ The Trick

It is Friday afternoon, the last Friday of the month, and the whole office is relaxed because it has achieved its targets and the pressure is off. You and your colleagues are all chatting, playing games on the computer or messing around with the photocopier. Your own conversation with Bobbie, the sales assistant, is interrupted by a paper ball that lands in your coffee. Elliott, the office joker, has decided it is time you entertained the department.

You walk over to him, wiping coffee from your shirt with a tissue and stand in front of him. 'Stand up, place your hands by your side and look me in the eye.' He does as you request.

'Let me ask if you believe you are your own man, an independent thinker, in charge of your own actions.' He nods and claims he is such a man.

'Then answer me this. Why did you obey my command and stand to attention without question or a moment's hesitation?'

Elliott looks uncomfortable and mumbles some excuse. The others giggle a little. You touch him warmly on the shoulder. 'Don't worry, I was simply playing with you. We can all forget ourselves and let someone or something else take control. Let me show you all.'

You instruct everybody to put their hands together as if praying, then to mesh their fingers and fold them down (*see* page 66).

'If you were to try and separate your hands now, you could do so with great ease. I am, however, going to convince you that your hands have become locked together – locked together so tightly that you could not possibly take them apart, at least not without severely damaging your hands. I will count slowly from one to twenty. With every number that I count, you will feel your hands becoming locked together, tighter and tighter, until you will not be able to take them apart at all. Do not squeeze your hands too much now. Just listen to me as I count from one to twenty and feel your hands begin to grip tighter and tighter.

'One, two, three – feel those hands gradually locking together. Four, five, six – tighter and tighter still – so tight that you will not be able to pull them apart. They will feel just as if locked together.

'Seven, eight, nine – feel them grip tighter. You can almost feel that glue, a very strong glue, is oozing between your fingers and bonding them together even tighter and tighter.'

As you say this, you run your finger across the tops of a few hands so if as to simulate the flow of a really strong glue.

'Ten, eleven – the grip between your fingers is really tight now. Tighter and tighter still. Feel that tension binding your hands together so tightly that you will hurt yourself if you try to pull them apart.

'Twelve, thirteen, fourteen – feel that glue all over, binding your hands and fingers tightly, tighter than anything you have experienced before.'

Run your fingers over some more hands, like glue again.

'Fifteen – really tight now. Sixteen, seventeen – tighter and tighter. Eighteen, nineteen, twenty. Your hands are now firmly fixed and I urge you to keep them still for just a moment.' You pause for a few seconds.

'Now very carefully, I want you to try and separate your hands. Do not force them, just try very, very carefully.'

Johnny, the office manager, and one or two others slowly manage to take their hands apart. But most people, including Elliott and Bobbie, seem to be stuck.

'You see, it is possible for you to forget your will and allow another mind to take complete control.'

Bobbie is beginning to look a little worried. 'I expect you would like me to release you.' They all nod.

'Very well. I shall deal with you each in turn. I shall touch your locked hands and count down from five to zero and your hands will be released.'

You turn to Bobbie, place your hand on hers and slowly count down. She cautiously takes her hands apart and thanks you.

You release your remaining colleagues, leaving Elliott until last, of course.

✧ Behind the Scenes

There is nothing hidden in this trick. What you see is what you get. In simple terms, it is an example of auto-suggestion, or perhaps mind over matter.

It is the repetitive words and the continuing suggestion that their hands will lock together that many people respond to. Although this is not in itself hypnosis, a similar technique is sometimes used by stage hypnotists to pick out those most susceptible to hypnotic suggestion from their audience.

However, the true effect of this trick in mind control cannot be achieved simply by repeating the script above. Certain other requirements are necessary.

The conditions in the room need to be just right. You must ensure that you can be the centre of attention for this to work, so an extremely busy environment, with lots going on, would not be suitable. It should be pleasantly warm, not too bright and, of course, have no loud music.

The attitude of your audience needs to be right. They should feel relaxed, not just in themselves and in the environment, but also with you. If they are too relaxed or quite tired, they might drop off to sleep. If they are artificially relaxed, with a few drinks inside them, they could be prone to disruption.

Your attitude needs to be right. You should be firm and in control, keeping your voice clear and even. Do not alter your tone or volume at all. Try to make your words rhythmic. Rock your audience into submission, as if they are babies and you are singing a gentle lullaby.

✶ The Performance

Once all the ingredients are right, it is then a matter of repeating the script above. Yes, it is repetitive, but that is intentional.

Touching the group's hands with yours when you talk about the glue cements the image of them being bonded together. Move about your audience, making strong eye contact with each of them in turn. As you look in their eyes, nod your head slowly, as if to give further affirmation. Take it slowly and watch the mind magic work itself.

Each person in your audience will react differently, as human beings all have different levels of suggestibility. One or two may experience only a small effect. Most will experience something, and some will be so tightly locked that they will never think of you in the same light again.

Releasing the hands is straightforward. You can either do this in a group or one at a time. Placing your hand over theirs is a nice touch, but not necessary. They will release their hands when you tell them to. After all, you are in control.

✶ Final Thoughts

Just like a stage hypnotist, I use this technique to find useful subjects for my demonstrations. I want to give the impression that a later part of my routine is mind control, so I use this trick to find a suitable helper. It is all a ruse, but please don't tell anyone.

One more thing to remember: don't do as I once did with a whole audience and forget to have them release their hands…

★ ★ ★ HOBSON'S CHOICE ★ ★ ★

Some people can't help doing as you say, no matter how hard they try.

Here is a further experiment in mind control. This time you are not controlling the audience's physiology, but rather their subconscious and their ability to make free choices. Of course, that is what you will appear to do. In fact, you employ a different variation of a technique already used in this book. This is not a ploy to cut corners, but actually demonstrates that techniques can be used in many ways. This, I hope, will lead you on to create new mind magic of your own.

This trick is built up in two stages, which adds a little drama and also helps to hide your methods. When your audience comes to recall these events in the future, it will have a magnified impression of your amazing abilities.

You will need

★ *Your written prediction.*

★ *Six everyday office items.*

★ *A smattering of magic.*

☀ The Trick

Elliott is dispatched to make more coffee. Johnny, the manager, thanks you for putting Elliott in his place.

'Oh, that wasn't my intention at all,' you say, giving a wry smile. 'I try to treat everyone equally, but I see you were not as susceptible as the others. Perhaps that's why you are the boss.'

Johnny knows you are joking.

'Mind you, I'm sure I could control your mind, given the opportunity. Maybe we should have a small wager.'

After some negotiation, it is agreed that Johnny will buy the beers tonight if you can demonstrate control over his mind. If not, the beers are on you.

'Bobbie, would you do me a favour and pass over the stapler, hole punch and ruler from your desk, please?'

You place the items in front of Johnny. You then write something on a piece of paper, fold it and give it to Bobbie to hold. You announce that this is your prediction of how Johnny will behave under your control.

You then look Johnny directly in the eye and say, 'I want you to relax and let my thoughts into your mind. In a moment I will ask you to select one of the three objects on the desk in front of you by elimination. You may think you have a free choice, but this is not the case. I have already made the choice for you. When I stop speaking, I want you to push two of the items away from you.'

Johnny pauses for a moment, looking at the objects. His hands move forward and push the ruler and hole punch away.

'Very good. This leaves us with the stapler. Bobbie, will you read out the note I just gave you, please?'

She confirms that you predicted the stapler.

There is a ripple of applause from around the office. It seems the boss is going to buy the drinks. The excitement, however, is short-lived. Johnny complains that the result was a fluke, a one-in-three chance, and is not happy. He wants something more challenging.

'Very well. Bobbie, could you also bring over a pencil, an eraser and that calculator.'

The objects are placed in a line on the desk in front of Johnny. You stand on the opposite side of the desk to him.

'So now, Johnny, you have a free choice from number one to six. What do you choose? Four. Are you certain? You may change your mind if you wish.' He indicates that he wishes to stick with four.

'Will you please count, starting from the left, from one to four? The ruler is at position four, so you have chosen the ruler. You haven't checked your e-mails for a while, have you, Johnny?' He looks at his watch and disappears into his office.

A few minutes later you see a group of your colleagues gathered at the notice-board. They are reading an e-mail from you addressed to Johnny. It reads: 'Dear Johnny, I knew you wouldn't believe me when I made you choose the stapler, but I think the ruler proves the point.'

And handwritten below? A brief message from the boss: 'The drinks are on me!'

✨ Behind the Scenes

Both parts of this trick rely upon different types of force. The first works only for three items, and requires some precise handling to make it look smooth. The second, while apparently more effective, is a little easier to perform.

The 'three-in-one force' can take one of three basic routes. Your job as the mind magician is to guide it imperceptibly to the required conclusion.

Place three objects in front of you and decide which will be the force object. Direct your helper to choose by pushing away two of the objects. If he does so, leaving the force object, you are home and dry. Pick it up and say, 'You chose the stapler' or whatever.

If he pushes away the force object and one other, you must then ask him, 'Which of those two will you have?' If he names the force object, you are again in the clear. Pick it up and go into the patter, 'You chose…'

If, when you ask, 'Which of those two will you have?' he names the other object, you must then push that back towards him, alongside the object eliminated earlier. Then say, 'You have eliminated these two objects,' pointing at them, 'and have chosen the…' naming the force object.

Given that you have said this is a process of 'elimination', all three possible routes to the choice seem fair to the audience. But remember, all the action needs to be done smoothly, without hesitation, as if it were natural and what you would do every time. Stopping to think for a second breaks the illusion.

The second version of the trick uses the 'six-in-one force'. Spectators perceive the trick to be harder because it involves more numbers. In fact, it's a whole lot easier than the three-in-one force.

Place six objects in a line on a table. Ideally, you should be opposite your helper. Place the force object third from your left. Now ask for a number between one and six.

If one is chosen, you spell out the word O-N-E, counting one object for each letter and starting from the left. You will arrive at the force object in position three.

If two is chosen, do exactly the same, except spell/count T-W-O. Again, you arrive at the third position.

If three is chosen, simply count to three, counting from the left.

If four is chosen, change tactics. From your helper's perspective the force object is in position four if he were to count from the left. So ask him to count to four from his left.

If five is chosen, you do the same again, except that you ask your helper to spell/count F-I-V-E from his left so that he arrives at the force object.

Finally, if six is chosen, you spell/count S-I-X starting from your left.

✶ The Performance

Wherever you get the urge to perform this trick, take some time to look around for suitable objects, and also look for means of presenting your predictions.

From your perspective, the first force is the trickier of the two, but your audience sees the second as more difficult because it involves double the number of objects.

So start off with the three-in-one force. Make sure you speak clearly to your helper and to the audience. They must all be aware that he has a free choice and must understand what you have asked him to do, otherwise they could become confused.

It is essential to state, 'We will select an item by elimination.' If this is omitted or misunderstood, the choice will not be seen as fair.

Allow your helper to make his 'choice', then have your prediction read out. You are halfway home.

In our story the helper decided that the result could have been just a fluke. In the real world it's probable that your audience will be impressed and amazed, wager or not. Does this mean you should forget the second part of the trick? Not at all. If you are not challenged about the result, why not say to your helper: 'I know you thought that was clever, but it was only a choice out of three. It could have been pure chance. I would like to show you something even more challenging.'

It will make you seem a much stronger performer if you are seen as wanting to push the boundaries, so get a few more objects on the table and perform the six-in-one force. Run through the routine, reveal your prediction and take your well-deserved drink on the boss.

✶ Final Thoughts

You can have lots of fun choosing different ways to reveal your prediction. Notes in envelopes always work, while e-mail is a great idea, especially within an office. I have even heard of a mind-magician who put his predictions on a website. With so many methods of communication available, the means of revelation are limitless.

★ ★ ★ ★ FALLEN ANGELS ★ ★ ★ ★

You have already seen the amazing power of suggestion earlier in this chapter. In fact this gives you something of an advantage: you now know who is most likely to respond well if you try a little bit more mind control.

The following trick can be great fun. Indeed, I've heard people talk about it for months after experiencing it. They seem to enjoy recalling how they were unable to maintain one of the most human of poses – standing on their own two feet – when there wasn't even a drink in sight.

Actually, this is one trick where a little alcohol can be a great help to you, as long as you steer clear of it yourself. It has been known for a queue of willing victims to form in front of me all wanting to try this one out.

You will need

★ A gullible friend.

★ A special mind-control script.

★ A smattering of magic.

✦ The Trick

You are something of a hero in the office, having earned everybody a free drink. Elliott is back and remarks that you must be able to wow all the girls with your mind-control abilities.

Of course, you would never stoop so low, but you feel you ought to remind Elliott who is in control.

'Very well,' you announce. 'I will show you how to make someone fall helplessly into your arms.' Elliott's ears prick up. 'Now I wonder who I should choose… Bobbie? Or should I pick on somebody else?' Your eyes fix on Elliott. The yells and whoops from the floor give a unanimous vote in favour of Elliott.

'Would you come over here and stand in front of me, please?' He does so and, being slightly taller, tries to lean over you.

'Calm down and step back,' you say. 'Please listen carefully.'

You explain that in a moment or two you will ask him to close his eyes. When

he has done that you will lightly touch his temples and he will feel himself falling forwards. He will not be able to stop himself.

'Are you ready?' He nods, closes his eyes and you touch his temples very gently. For a moment nothing happens, but then he begins to waver, the motion becomes stronger and eventually he falls forward. You hold his shoulders and stop him falling.

You help Elliott to a chair, he looks you in the eye and thanks you for helping him.

You look at your watch. It's Friday evening – almost time you were in the pub with Michael and your friends…

✴ Behind the Scenes

This trick has much in common with 'Gripping Stuff' (see page 64).

In many ways, however, 'Fallen Angels' is even stronger, as it has the very dramatic effect of causing a fully grown adult to topple over. If you use 'Gripping Stuff' first and select a really good candidate for this, then you have a great piece of mind magic ready to perform.

'Fallen Angels' requires greater attention to detail than 'Gripping Stuff', and you really must focus on one person to make it work.

In choosing your helper, there are three points to consider:

Height: It helps if they are slightly taller than you are.

Attitude: If they seem open and willing, that is good. If they are cocky and in a 'prove it to me' kind of mood, they will not respond as well as you need.

Susceptibility: If you have checked this out with another trick beforehand, then so much the better.

You both should be standing, face to face. Ask your helper to remain straight and firm yet relaxed and flexible. Tell them to imagine that their ankles are like well-greased ball joints. Ask them to move freely as you gently attempt to pull them backwards and forwards.

If they move with ease and without real resistance, you are home and dry. If they do not, try again to get them to relax. If they still fail to relax, you might have to consider changing helpers.

You now look them in the eye and say, 'I want you to listen very carefully to what I am about to say.' You nod your head. 'For the moment I wish you to do nothing. Just stand still and listen to what I have to say. Do you understand?'

Your helper should nod.

'Very good. In a moment I will ask you to close your eyes. Do not do so just yet. When you have done so I will touch you lightly on the temples with my fingertips.' You touch your own temples to demonstrate. 'When I do this you will find yourself falling forwards into my arms. You will not be able to stop. You will not harm yourself for I will be here to catch you.' You nod at your helper.

'Once again, in a moment I will ask you to close your eyes. I will then touch your temples very gently with my fingertips.' You touch your own temples. 'You will then find yourself falling towards me.' You gesture towards yourself. 'But you will not come to any harm, I assure you.' Again you nod at them and they will nod back if all is well.

'Finally, then, I will ask you in a second to close your eyes, I will touch your temples and you will fall forwards. You will not be able to control this.

'Close your eyes, please.'

At this point you touch their temples lightly, and you will find in a few seconds, if you have chosen well, that they will fall gently into your arms. Be ready to catch them and hold them for a moment while they compose themselves.

✴ The Performance

There are just a few brief points to add about the performance.

Do choose a calm and easy environment for this trick.

Make your words calm and a little monotonous. You are trying to numb your helper's mind for a few moments.

Reassure your helper that they will not come to any harm. Point out any potential hazards, such as tables or chairs, and say how you will stand between them and the hazard.

When you have finished, play up the care you take of your helper. This will emphasize the impact of what you have just done.

✴ Final Thoughts

You have shown great powers of mind control, but these tricks are just for fun. Make sure you choose your helpers wisely, using people who will play along and who are unlikely to be easily distressed or injured. Certainly do not perform this for minors.

A NIGHT THAT GOES WITH A BUMP!

'A host is like a general: calamities often reveal his genius.'

HORACE (65–8 BC)

It was a dark cold night and the wind whistled loudly, violently banging doors and windows on its way down the street. A small group of people, frightened by the storm and by what lay ahead, stopped outside a gate and paused to catch their breath before entering.
They knocked on the door.
Footsteps grew louder and louder, then, with a blood-curdling creak, the door slowly opened. Chilling organ chords reverberated at ear-splitting volume. The figure at the door stared at the travellers and said, 'Hello, everyone. How are you all? Love the dress. Oh, a bottle of wine - you shouldn't have...'
The scene fades away.

Forgive the indulgent drama above, but I felt it would be worthwhile showing you how not to prepare people for your mind magic. Ideally, your guests should feel a pleasant sense of anticipation, not be frightened out of their wits.

You will have realised that the most important aspects of Mind Magic are timing and setting. A Paranormal Party makes a great setting and that's what we will look at here. Even if you never hold such a party, this chapter contains some important performance tips for you to consider.

★ ★ AN INVITATION TO THE DARKER SIDE ★ ★

So you have decided to hold a paranormal party. What's the best way to ensure your guests turn up? A really intriguing invitation, perhaps like the one below, will work wonders.

RAYMOND & KAREN

You are invited to an evening of the unusual
31 October - 8.00 p.m. till late (very late)
Dine on mysterious delicacies from around the globe
Spirits both liquid and ethereal in abundance
Dress: Dark
Hearses at 1.00 a.m.

PLEASE BRING THIS INVITATION WITH YOU

This will certainly cause interest and draw people in. What it will not do is scare people, as in this chapter's opening scenario.

If possible, prepare your invitations on a PC and print them out in portrait shape (longer edge vertical). If you keep just the names in the upper part and put the other details in the lower portion, you have an ideal set of cards to perform 'Death Becomes You', described later in the book.

✦ A Question of Character

Who will you be on the night of your party, or whenever you perform your mind magic? Unless you are performing publicly to an audience who does not know you well, there is really only one person you can be – you. If you are usually an outgoing, larger than life character, this is not a licence for you to be brash and lapse into slapstick comedy. Perhaps project the quieter, more reflective part of yourself – warm, humorous and friendly, but not a joker.

Dress smartly and fashionably, retaining dignity and decorum. Yellow shirts are most certainly out, while deep blues and reds are most certainly in.

Carry yourself through the evening in as relaxed a manner as you can, having

prepared as much as possible in advance. Know where everything is and have it to hand so that there is no need to panic. Ideally, keep all your props and paraphernalia in smart wooden boxes, or, in the case of everyday items, in their normal places in the home. Craft and New Age shops stock fine jewellery and trinket boxes, so pop in and have a look round. While there, you might also pick up some good ideas for creating the right atmosphere.

✳ Mood and Music

Getting the right ambience is perhaps the most important element of your party planning. As stressed throughout this book, mind magic is very much about the stories and experiences that you draw your audience into. If they are not comfortable and relaxed, they will not become absorbed so easily and your job becomes much harder.

Light as much of your home as you can with candles, and supplement these with subdued electric light. Turn on your table lamps and light your candelabra, but turn off any fluorescent lighting.

Although you want subtlety, take care that your performing area is reasonably well lit so that your guests can see what you are trying to show them.

The New Age trinket shops that seem to be everywhere these days are crammed full of small decorative items that can be picked up very reasonably. Placing a few of these around your home can help to set the scene, creating a background somewhat out of the ordinary.

Music is an enormously powerful tool for a mind-magician, and there are two ways in which you can make good use of it.

☀ Setting the mood

As your guests arrive, have some gentle but familiar music playing quietly. The choice is up to you, but obviously extended drum solos or Wagnerian opera may be a bit too distracting. Choose something that reflects you and your friends as much as possible – perhaps some moving classical pieces by Mahler, some jazz by Jacques Loussier, or some Gregorian chants.

☀ When you perform

Music not only provides a backdrop for your stories, but it can also act as a tool to help your audience become emotionally involved. It is important, however, that the music does not draw attention to itself, but rather sets the pace. There is a lot of music sold for relaxation purposes, and this is ideal.

☀ Soul Food

You will undoubtedly want your guests to eat, drink and be merry, so try to make the food and drink as exotic as possible. A formal meal may be too ambitious, so keep to finger foods that can be eaten throughout the evening. Asian and Oriental delicacies are great as there are so many to choose from, and a self-service buffet will free you up to entertain your guests.

If you're feeling creative, try making some snacks in unusual shapes. (I have some pastry-cutters shaped like the signs of the zodiac.) Find out what you can get hold of locally, then make sandwiches, vol-au-vents or whatever you like into shapes that reflect a particular theme.

On a cold night there is nothing better than to be welcomed with a glass of hot mulled wine. This wonderful brew is a traditional English favourite made from red wine infused with lemons and spices. It relaxes people nicely and is a great conversation opener. Look for a recipe in your local library or on the Internet.

★ ★ ★ ★ PARANORMAL PLAYTIME ★ ★ ★ ★

If you were to fill your evening with mind magic alone, your guests would become bored very quickly. To add variety, why not try playing some of the 'games' suggested below?

✦ Blind Man's Buffet

This game is played in pairs. One person from each pair is blindfolded and given a notepad and pen. The sightless contestants sit in a row with their partner in front of them and they must all remain absolutely silent.

You bring in six dishes containing various foodstuffs in unusual combinations. Try to choose things that have interesting textures, such as the following:

• Kiwi fruit with ketchup
• Sausagemeat with maple syrup
• Taramasalata on chocolate biscuits

You get the idea. Experiment to your heart's content, but make sure that everything is cooked or can be eaten raw.

Now each blindfolded individual is spoonfeed a little of each food in turn by their companion. The object of the game is for them to write on the pad what they think they have tasted.

This is fun because it combines suspense with humour. There is great hilarity in trying to read what has been written by several nauseated people who have been temporarily blinded. It is also a good starting point to talk about perception, and thus can lead you into an opportunity to show some mind magic.

✦ Blind Man's Surprise

Here's a little variation on the previous game that you can use to play a slightly wicked trick on someone.

When you have totalled the scores, you announce that Karen, the winner, gets to play a special game. She remains blindfolded and you announce that a few of your guests will stand behind her and touch her forehead. Her job is to guess who is who.

Several people take turns and touch her head. She gets one or two correct, but most are wrong. 'You're doing well,' you say, 'but can you guess this one?'

You walk behind her yourself, and as you touch her, she screams and jumps out of the chair.

How to do it

Well, you need a glass of mulled wine and a bag of ice or some other frozen object. You also have a card with the words: 'Please warm your hands on the wine glass before playing.'

Make sure your victim is blindfolded and tell everyone they must remain silent. Hand the card and wine glass to the first person to be guessed. Make sure they warm their hands for a few seconds.

While as many people as you can muster touch your victim in turn, you take the opportunity to chill your hands on the ice bag. When it is your turn, the difference will be literally shocking.

✦ Who Robbed the Ferryman?

This isn't actually a game, although it is played as such. It is, in fact, a little stunt that you can learn very easily.

You ask Paul to step forward. You take a handful of coins out of your pocket and count them into Paul's hand. You gesture for him to hand the coins back to you.

'Paul, I have seven coins with which we can play a little game. In a moment I will again count them one

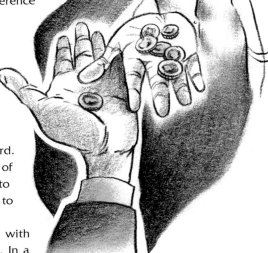

at a time into your hand. As soon as the seventh coin is counted, I want you to close your hand as quickly and tightly as you can. I will try and spirit one coin away. Your job is to stop me doing so. Do you understand?' He nods.

You begin counting the coins into his open palm with your right hand: 'One, two, three, four, five, six, seven.'

As Paul closes his fist on the coins, your left hand passes under his and produces one of the coins. Paul checks in his hand: there are only six coins.

'You didn't do very well that time, but it was your first go. Let's try again.'

You take back the coins and count them again. Paul is even quicker this time, but still you manage to spirit a coin from his hand.

After two more tries, Paul gives up. Is this an example of mind over matter?

How to do it

This game is great fun, and you can play it at any time. What happens is this. You hold the coins in your left hand and take them one at a time in your right hand and count them into your helper's hand. When you get to number six, you don't take a coin, you just go through the motions. You then carry on and count seven, taking a coin and placing it in his hand.

If you do this in a steady rhythm, especially with no change in pace at number six, your ruse will go unnoticed. The victim is too busy concentrating on closing his hand sharply and beating you to notice that there is a coin missing from his hand and that you still have one in yours.

✨ Final Thoughts

Whatever you do at your party, there is one thing to bear in mind: everyone must have fun. So make your guests feel welcome, feed and water them generously, and entertain them well.

You might want to shock them a little and keep them in suspense from time to time, but you should steer away from scaring them too much. Mind-magicians walk in a dark, unusual world, where some things cannot be explained with ease. We do not walk in a world of fear and horror – we would be crazy to put ourselves, or anyone else, through that.

We live in a world of mystery and magic, and to finish your party off, I suggest you perform the truly amazing tricks in the final chapter.

DROP DEAD MAGIC

'Man dies of cold, not of darkness.'

MIGUEL DE UNAMUNO (1864–1936)

It is often said in show business that you should always leave your audience wanting more, and one can hardly argue with that point. What can also be said for a magical performance is that the closing items should have the greatest impact.

Mind Magic should have the power to mystify and intrigue, as well as to unnerve and shock. It would be easy to leave our audiences disturbed by what we show them. But if we do that then surely our motives must be wrong. People enjoy being scared on roller-coasters - but only because they know the ride will not last long. Our magic can be powerful and must be used wisely.

In this closing chapter are two tricks, both very powerful, which you could use to close any performance of mind magic. While there is a little work required to prepare and perform them, this is outweighed by the impact they will have.

I hope you enjoy them both.

★ ★ ★ ★ DEATH BECOMES YOU ★ ★ ★ ★

The stunning impact this trick has on the audience is acheived by combining a force to create the effect of precognition by a spirit who sends a mystifying message to one of your guests. This trick uses a principle described earlier in the book, but with an extra something to create a real shock factor.

You will need

★ A stack of specially prepared invitation cards.

★ A special card.

★A large group of fifteen or more friends.

★ A smattering of magic.

✴ The Trick

As each guest arrives at your party, take care to have them hand you their original invitation. Keep those you have collected in a pile bound together with a rubber band.

After all the food has been eaten and all the games have been played, people once again ask you to demonstrate some mind magic.

'Very well,' you say. 'But what I have to show you now will shock you all, and one of you in particular. So for those who are of a nervous disposition, I suggest you retire to the kitchen.'

You begin to clear your dining table to make some space, and your friends help.

'Gather round. Helen, would you be kind enough to pass me that pile of invitation cards from the mantelpiece?' You turn to the man on your right.

'Felix, do you recognize this card?' you ask, pointing towards the invitation that is on top of the stack. Felix nods, as this is the invitation card he received and handed back to you earlier.

'Very good. I need twelve of these cards, which I shall number on the back.'

You take the card out of the stack and write the number 12 boldly on the back. You continue this process, writing out a further ten cards, numbering them as you go. Finally, you turn to John, your brother.

'John, do you recognize this card?' He nods, and you turn the card over and mark it number one.

You now carefully arrange the cards in a clock-face formation and ask the owners of the cards to stand around the table adjacent to their card.

'Now we can begin. Many priests and other religious men will warn you against the dangers of meddling with the supernatural. They will tell you that such activities, if not controlled properly, can summon evil spirits, which can bring harm and leave innocent people cursed.

'Tonight we will perform a small ritual – one known for centuries to ancient mystics. A ritual in which the spirits choose a soul to take.' You explain that for this ritual you need a beautiful young woman.

'Helen, I will now give you the choice of any one of the twelve men here.' She giggles a little. 'Please make a mental selection of the man you choose and the number of his card. I want you to spell that number out in your mind, walking around the circle as you do so. Count one person for each letter, starting of course with the person at card number one. I will turn my back so I cannot see what you are doing.'

Helen silently walks around the circle, touching each person's shoulder as she goes. She tells you she has finished.

'Good. Now I want you to note the number of the person you have stopped at and spell that number out in the same way, starting with the next person.'

Once again, she walks around slowly and tells you she is done.

'For the third time, please repeat the process, spelling the number on the person's card you are now stopped at. When you are done, I want you to stop and touch the person you have finished at on the shoulder.'

She follows your request and comes to rest, touching John lightly on the shoulder.

You turn back. 'John! Don't look now, but is that your invitation card in front of you?' He nods.

'And when did you last see the face of that card? Just before I laid it down in front of you, is that correct?' He nods again.

'Can you recall what was on the card?' John explains that it was addressed to him and simply told where and when the party would be.

'Very good. We may now see if our ritual has called the spirits forward. Will you all, except John, turn over your cards?'

As people do so, they see that they are now all blank, save for their names written at the top. The eleven helpers and those watching murmur in disbelief.

You look towards John and nod at his card. He turns it over. Below his name there is an inscription written in red: 'You are the chosen one – we invite you to join us again soon.'

You look at John, shrug your shoulders and give a wry smile. You retire gracefully from the room.

✴ Behind the Scenes

There are two secrets employed in making this trick work. The first is the force of the number 1, as demonstrated in 'Astronome' (*see* page 51). The second makes use of some specially prepared cards. In fact, the invitation cards used in the story are not the ones collected during the evening.

You need to prepare a second set of cards that looks similar to the invitation cards. They should have a space along the top in which you write the name of your guest, as on the real invites.

The lower part of the cards, where the party details would be, is left blank – except, of course, the one used for John, which has the message written on it. Write the message in red ink in a shaky ghostly hand for best effect. Place John's card at the twelfth position, and have a few blank cards left underneath.

Now comes the sneaky part. You have a piece of card half the size of the others made from the bottom part of a real invitation. This is placed on top of the pile of cards and a rubber band placed around the middle to cover the join. The top card therefore looks like the original invitation and you can show it as such. If you slide it out of the pack with its back to your audience, no one will ever know it's a fake.

✦ The Performance

As your guests arrive, make a point of asking for their invitation cards. During the ensuing conversation, ask one or two of them, 'Did I take your invitation card yet?' As you collect the cards, keep them together with a rubber band. Later, in a quiet moment, hide them away and place your prepared stack of cards on the mantelpiece.

When the time comes to perform, make a big fuss about having to make space for the demonstration. Gather your guests around and have your stack of cards handed to you. Go through the process of showing everyone the front of their card, turning the pack over, removing the card and writing a number from twelve down to one on the back. What your guests will apparently see are their twelve invitation cards being marked on the back and placed in front of them. Of course, you must make sure you don't show the front of the cards after they have been removed.

Now have a thirteenth person go through the counting process. Instruct them to do this quietly, touching each person they count on the shoulder as they pass by.

Ask all but the chosen person to turn over their cards together. There will be a brief hubbub while the impact of the cards being blank sinks in. Now is the time to ask your chosen guest to turn over his or her card...

The rest is, as they say, up to you.

✦ Final Thoughts

It almost goes without saying that you should choose a strong character to be your chosen victim in this trick. Someone of a nervous disposition might take it too literally and become quite distressed.

If you do not have invitation cards for your party, you could simply make up a stack of cards with names at the top and another symbol at the bottom, such as a question mark or pentacle. Remember, you have to draw this only once on the half-card.

A closing thought about your victim on the night: before he leaves for home you might want to take him to one side and whisper in his ear, 'It was only a trick.'

★ ★ ★ ★ FAMOUS LAST WORDS ★ ★ ★ ★

One of the classical forms of mind magic is a trick called 'Book Test'. The typical plot is that the mind-magician asks a helper to choose a page in a book. The magician is then able to determine words of sentences from the book using his mystical powers.

Although this trick has been used by magicians for over a hundred years, it remains as deceptive today as it ever was.

Given the correct setting, the right choice of book and a well-acted performance, this trick makes a fitting end to your journey into the world of mind magic.

You will need

★ *A paperback book. (A horror novel is ideal).*

★ *A sketch-book and a marker pen.*

★ *A smattering of magic.*

✶ The Trick

It is late in the evening and your living room has become noticeably cooler. Your guests are waiting patiently, wondering what you have been doing for the last few minutes.

You return carrying a sketchpad and a paperback novel, and place them on the table.

'Before you all go, I wish to give you one last demonstration – one that I do not attempt very often for it is tiring and sometimes does not work that well. Nonetheless, I am willing to put myself at risk of exhaustion and embarrassment on this occasion.'

You take the book from the table, flick through it and look up at your expectant audience. 'This book was published in 1897. It contains various accounts of some ordinary people and their encounters with a strange and mysterious host. Rather fitting for our gathering this evening, I think.

'Some of you may know the book, or have seen some of the amusing movie interpretations. It is, however, a classic of the bizarre. I present to you *Dracula* by Bram Stoker.'

You cast your eyes around the room in order to select your helper. Following John's recent experience, many of your guests avoid making eye contact with you.

'Jason, you have always been the studious type. You can quickly get to grips with a passage of words and interpret their real meaning. I would like you to help.'

You beckon Jason towards you and ask him to sit in the chair next to you. You stand in front of him.

'In a moment I want you to choose a page in this book. You should do this completely at random. I will flick through the pages and when you feel the moment is right, I want you to call out "Stop". Do you understand?'

He nods, so you promptly flick through the pages of the book from back to front. He calls you to stop perhaps two-thirds of the way through the book. You insert your finger at the stopping point and turn your head so you cannot possibly glimpse the words on that page.

'Are you happy to use this page or shall we select another?' Jason indicates that he would like to use that page.

'Very well. Take the book, please and open it up at the page you stopped on. Now find the first new paragraph starting on that page. You have it? Good. Now read that paragraph over and over to yourself. Do not mouth the words – just read them in your mind, please.'

Jason begins to look intently at the words in the book, his eyes scanning the lines over and over.

You take up your sketchpad and pen, and without a word you begin to draw, a little slowly at first. Occasionally you pause and look at your reader.

'I am just working to get an image from your mind. The more you re-read those 100-year-old words, the clearer the image will be and the easier for me to pick up. I will keep on trying.'

Eventually you come to a stop. You take one last look at Jason and another at your drawing. You prop up the drawing on your mantelpiece for all to see, then move to a chair on the other side of the room and wearily sit down.

Your guests take a look at the drawing. It depicts a church on a hillside. Beside the church is a man. He is dressed smartly in a black suit and wears a tall black hat. Beside him is a lady in a Victorian-style dress. They are both somewhat out of proportion to the church.

In the foreground are two gravestones, but they stand by empty graves, which are obviously awaiting the arrival of their occupants. And beside each grave is a coffin waiting to be interred.

One gravestone is engraved with the name Lucy.

'Jason, I know by now you must be fed up with reading that passage, but I would like you to read it one last time – aloud so all can hear.'

'The funeral was arranged for the next succeeding day, so that Lucy and her mother might be buried together. I attended to all the ghastly formalities, and the urbane undertaker proved that his staff was afflicted, or blessed, with something of his own obsequious suavity. Even the woman who performed the last offices for the dead remarked to me, 'She makes a very beautiful corpse, sir. It's quite a privilege to attend on her. It's not too much to say that she will do credit to our establishment!'

As Bram Stoker's words are read aloud, your guests see that they describe a scene identical to the one they observed you create. Small gasps and murmurs are heard as each individual comes to realize that they have witnessed a most amazing feat.

Your brother hands you a glass of wine; you've earned it. He calls everyone to attention.

'Friends, please raise your glasses to our incredible mind-magician.'

✦ Behind the Scenes

This impressive trick is no more than a force, just like the card force you learned at the beginning of this book (*see* page 13).

In this case you force a particular page in the book while appearing to give your helper the opportunity to pick entirely at random. This is achieved through a very well-proven yet incredibly deceptive 'modification' to your chosen novel.

First, of course, you must choose your book. Paperbacks certainly work better than hardbacks, but either can be used. Spend some time thinking about the book to use. A piece of classic horror, as in the story above, is one option, but perhaps a more modern factual book, or another style of novel, might suit you better. Whatever you choose, make sure it is of substantial length and has fairly dense writing. This way you can't be accused of using memory or taking a sneaky peek to pull the trick off.

Once you have chosen your book, you need to decide which page to use. Choose one about a third of the way into the book, and make sure it has a passage containing a very strong visual element. 'He walked into the room to find…' could come from almost any book you pick off the shelf, so choose something a little unusual and in keeping with the main theme of the book.

If the passage creates a memorable image in your own mind, it's perfect because you can draw what's in your head. Practise drawing the image until you can do so with ease: this will allow you to concentrate on your presentation.

One final point: ideally, the words you want to use should be on a left-hand page. This will make the book a lot easier for you to handle when you execute the force.

Now comes the sneaky part – the modification of the book. Open the book at the selected page, take a pair of scissors and cut a small triangle from the bottom right-hand corner of the opposite page as in the diagram. Now, if you take the book and riffle through from back to front with your thumb on the bottom right-hand corner of the book, you will see that (given a little practice) you can successfully halt at the desired force page.

Practise riffling through slowly, and enlist the help of a friend to call out 'Stop' at random. You will find you are apparently able to stop at his command, while in fact stopping at the force page.

Once you have mastered this technique, you are ready to stun your audience by performing an amazing feat.

✦ The Performance

Gather your audience around and select your helper for this trick. It is essential to have some control of their actions because you don't want them flicking through the book again when you have already forced the page. So sit them down, stand in front of them and clearly take command.

Hold your book and explain a little about it, maybe saying how many pages it has and perhaps having someone look at several pages to confirm that the book has not been tampered with in any way.

Explain to your helper that you wish them to say 'Stop' when you riffle through the book, demonstrating this yourself by exclaiming 'Stop' about halfway through. This will show them what they have to do and indicate they should not wait for ever before calling out.

Execute the force as described above, putting your finger in the chosen page to make sure it is not lost when you hand over the book. Turning your head here not only reinforces the idea that you can't read the page, but also that you don't know where in the book your helper stopped.

Ask the helper to read through the passage and pick up your pad to begin drawing. Don't rush this; take your time, as if receiving the image slowly, bit by bit. Make the drawing clear and to the point, not too fussy.

When the work is done, put the picture on show and ask the helper to read the passage aloud.

✦ Final Thoughts

Two thoughts occur to me about this wonderful trick. First, it could be described as a premonition rather than a mind-reading feat by having the drawing already and secreted in an envelope. You could even make a painting and describe how it has been handed down through the generations.

The second thought is that you could perform this trick off the cuff at a friend's house if you can get hold of the book beforehand. I am not suggesting you mutilate your friend's property, but you could make a force page simply by folding a corner backwards which can be corrected later.

GLOSSARY

Astrology
The study of the positions of celestial bodies, and their influence on the course of our daily lives.

Cartomancy
Fortune-telling using cards, possibly Tarot Cards or regular playing cards.

Clairvoyance/Clairaudience
The ability to perceive, hear or see events or facts remotely.

Divination
Foretelling future events or revealing knowledge by psychic means.

Effect
What you intend your audience to perceive when they watch a magic trick performed.

Force
A set-up or ruse controlled by you that causes your helper to choose the item you wish, whilst giving the impression they have had a free choice.

Gimmicked
An object secretly modified in some way for the purposes of performing magic.

Helper
The person or persons from your audience that you choose to assist you in your performance.

Hypnotism
The science of causing a human mind to enter a deep state of subconscious where it becomes more susceptible to suggestion and influence.

Mentalism
The branch of magic or conjuring related to mind-reading effects.

Misdirection
Diverting your audience's attention so that secret moves or set-ups go unnoticed.

Palmistry
Fortune-telling and divination using the lines on the human hand.

Patter
The words a magician uses to accompany his performance. They help to provide a setting, a context and mis-direction.

Precognition
Advance knowledge, usually by psychic means, of an event, thought, reaction etc. before it occurs.

Psychic
A person capable of mental feats such as extrasensory perception. A general term for anyone who is 'gifted'. The word is derived from the ancient Greek word for the soul.

Psychometry
The ability to garner information about an object and its owner by psychic means.

Psychokinesis/Telekinesis
The ability to cause objects to move by thought or psychic power.

Spirit
The vital force within living beings or the soul believed to depart from the body of a person at death. Also an angel or a demon.

Tarot Cards
A style of playing card of ancient origin used for fortune-telling and prediction.

Telepathy
Communication through means other than the normal five senses, for example by psychic means, our sixth sense.

TRICKS OF THE TRADE

Every magician knows that if you are not correctly prepared you may make mistakes. This would be a pity as it would dampen both your enthusiasm to perform and that of your audience to watch you in the future. So below are some simple rules for you to follow to help you perform your Mind Magic in the most professional way possible.

☀ Rule 1

Practice makes perfect. In the same way actors have to learn their lines or musicians must learn their scales, so magicians must learn their tricks inside out. You may have heard budding magicians advised to practise in front of a mirror. This is good advice for those developing intricate sleight-of-hand skills. There is little if any such complex detail in this book. However, you should become familiar with the tricks, the order of events, your words or 'patter' and all the objects and props you will be using. You should also give thought to where you position yourself and your audience and particularly to where any helpers will be throughout your performance.

In other words, get organized. Make sure you know where everything and everyone will be during your performance.

☀ Rule 2

Never repeat a trick to the same audience. When you have just performed a minor miracle, as I know you will do given plenty of practice, the immediate cry from your audience will be, 'That was great! Show us again.' No doubt you will be tempted to do so, given the applause you have just received. Who wouldn't want more of that?!

This is a temptation you must resist. The effect is never the same second time around. So it is better to show them a different effect when you are ready to do so. You must also know when to stop as people can get bored of the incessant chant, 'Here's another, watch this!'

There is a good reason for not repeating your tricks: given a second viewing your audience is more likely to be able to work out how it was done and the mystery will vanish before their eyes.

☀ Rule 3

Never reveal your methods to anyone other than other magicians. You may say to me, 'Hang on, aren't you doing just that in this book?' In fact I am not, for, you see, to fully understand these tricks and their working requires you to read the book and pay it some significant attention. This means you are interested enough to qualify as a magician. After all we are all magicians at heart with varying levels of knowledge and ability.

I hope you find the book enjoyable to read as I have done my best to describe the Mind Magic in realistic settings and include 'real people'. Of course, when performing, you do not need to recreate these settings absolutely. You should take the tricks in this book, fit them into your world and make them very much your own.

WHAT NEXT?

FURTHER READING

Many great books on magic have been published, and as the rules and principles of magic remain constant, they date very slowly. The following is a list of titles for you to consider.

✳ General Magic Books

Christopher Milbourne, *The Illustrated History Of Magic*, Robert Hale

Karl Fulves, *Self Working Card Magic*, Dover Publications

Karl Fulves, *Self Working Table Magic*, Dover Publications

Jean Hugard, *Modern Magic Manual*, Dover Publications

Richard Jones, *That's Magic!*, New Holland

Mark Wilson, *Complete Course in Magic*, Blitz

✳ Mind Magic & Mentalism

Theodore Anneman, *Practical Mental Magic*, Dover Publications

Eugene Burger, *Mastering The Art Of Magic*, Kaufmann & Co

Tony Corrinda, *13 Steps To Mentalism*, Robbins Publishers

Karl Fulves, *Self Working Mental Magic*, Dover Publications

Barrie Richardson, *Theater Of The Mind*, Hermetic Press

Reginald Scot, *The Discoverie Of Witchcraft*, Dover Publications

T.A Waters, *Mind, Myth & Magick*, Hermetic Press

USEFUL ADDRESSES

Here are some useful addresses of dealers in all things magic, magazines and societies who will be only too pleased to help. I start with my own website.

www.mind-magic.info

✳ Magic Dealers

Alakazam Magic
Unit 113
Ellingham Industrial Park
Ellingham Way
Ashford
Kent TN 23 6LZ
United Kingdom
www.readminds.co.uk

International Magic
89 Clerkenwell Road
London EC1R 5BX
United Kingdom
www.internationalmagic.com

Hank Lee's Magic Factory,
PO Box 789
Medford
MA 02155
USA
www.hanklee.com

✳ Magic Magazines

Magic Week – an online newsletter updated weekly
www.magicweek.com

Genii Magazine
P.O. Box 36038
Los Angeles
CA 90036
USA

INDEX

DEDICATION

For Catherine

ACKNOWLEDGEMENTS

Firstly, thanks to Jo at New Holland for being mad enough to give this project a go and to Camilla for all her help and guidance through the process of putting this book together.

To my closest magical friends Graeme Middleton and Andrew Paul, who showed faith in me when I needed it most; with special thanks to Andrew for his help, criticism, guidance and inspiration in the technical aspects of much of the material.

Finally, to all magicians, past, present and future whose attitudes, inventions, creativity and performances have led me, be it by inspiration, motivation or by my deliberate avoidance of their thinking, to create the magic and philosophy present in this book.